'1976' H/. £5/R

376

The Road
to Yorktown

JOHN SELBY

The Road to Yorktown

The surrender at Yorktown was the real climax of
the war. There, in 1781, the end of the road which
the Americans had started off along from
Lexington in 1775 was reached

HAMISH HAMILTON

LONDON

First published in Great Britain 1976
by Hamish Hamilton Ltd
90 Great Russell Street London WC1B 3PT

Copyright © 1976 by John Selby

SBN 241 89293 7

Photoset, printed and bound
in Great Britain by
REDWOOD BURN LIMITED
Trowbridge & Esher

CONTENTS

ILLUSTRATIONS

Chapter One

WASHINGTON

'No one at the outset showed any disposition to attribute to him any great
military qualities, but all appeared to admire him for his rectitude, sound
judgment and business experience. Eliphalet Dyer probably spoke the
mind of many when he announced that Washington was highly esteemed
by those who knew him, but "as to military and real service he knows no
more than some of ours". In the end expedience to assure Southern support seems to have prevailed even though the impression of
Washington's martial ability had failed to convince that he was preeminently the man to head the army.'

The Congress at Philadelphia—15 June 1775

GEORGE WASHINGTON gained his military experience, such as it was,
on a number of expeditions to the Ohio. When he first visited the region
its inhabitants were Seneca Mingos under Half King Tanachristan. By
this time white traders from the English colonies—mostly Pennsylvanians who reckoned the region part of Penn's Woods—had drifted in.
They provided manufactured goods in exchange for furs, and made a
good profit thereby; they were the first whites other than the early French
explorers to penetrate the region. Inevitably they clashed with the French
whose posts stretched from the Great Lakes down to the mouth of the
Mississippi. As the Indians tended to side with whoever provided the best
goods, a bitter struggle began for the domination of the Indian trade. This
was intensified when, besides lone traders, merchant trading companies
appeared on the scene. Among the latter was the Ohio Company whose
directors included Lawrence and Augustine Washington, older half-
brothers of George. Later, Lieutenant-Governor Dinwiddie of Virginia
became a partner.

Not willing to brook this competition the French in 1749 sent a military force to assert their authority. They subsequently ordered the English
out of the area, took prisoner any traders caught there, and began to build
a string of forts to consolidate their hold.

The Pennsylvanian legislature, dominated by Quakers, had already

I

refused their Governor money to set up a post on the Ohio. This resolute French action dissuaded others from the Colony from trying to trade and settle in the Ohio valley. The Virginians, however, were more persistent. The Ohio Company obtained a grant of land from the Mingos and decided to establish a post by the Ohio Forks.[1] The Company set up a store on the bank of the upper Potomac opposite Wills Creek and had a wagon road cut to the warehouse which had been built by its agent William Trent on Redstone Creek, halfway towards the Forks. Trent was also given a captain's commission and told to enlist an infantry company of his fellow traders and frontiersmen to protect the workmen who would build the fort.

Other places of call in the area at that time were Christopher Gist's settlement beyond Chestnut Ridge, and John Frazier's post where he repaired guns and tools for the Indians. Frazier had been established on French Creek in the north, until driven away by the advancing French. He was now settled on Turtle Creek a few miles south of the Forks.

*

When news reached Virginia that the French were on the move and occupying forcibly the valley of the Ohio to which the Colony believed it had a rightful claim, Dinwiddie, who was doubly involved as Lieutenant-Governor of Virginia and a partner in the Ohio Company, decided to take action. His first move was to write a letter of protest addressed to the commandant of the French forces on the Ohio. This was entrusted to George Washington, a newly commissioned officer in the Virginia Militia. The opening paragraph shows clearly the Governor's views on the matter:

> The lands upon the River Ohio in the western parts of the colony of Virginia are so notoriously known to be the property of the Crown of Great Britain that it is a matter of equal surprise and concern to me to hear that a body of French forces are erecting fortresses and making settlements upon the river within His Majesty's Dominions. The many and repeated complaints I have received of these acts of hostility lay me under the necessity of sending in the name of the King my master the bearer here of George Washington Esq. one of the Adjutants General[2] of the Forces of this Dominion to complain to you of the encroachments thus made, and of the injuries done to the subjects of Great Britain in open violation of the Laws of Nations and the treaties subsisting between the two Crowns . . .

To carry out his mission Washington assembled in November 1753 at

[1] The junction of the Allegheny and Monongahela rivers.

[2] The death of Lawrence Washington in 1752, who was an Adjutant General of Virginia, had left vacant one of the four militia adjutancies. George Washington applied for and obtained the post which gave him £150 p.a. and the rank of major.

Washington on the Ohio, by Charles Willson Peale

Wills Creek a party consisting of frontiersman Christopher Gist, four assistants, two of whom were seasoned Indian traders, and a French interpreter. They set out on 15 November on horseback with pack-animals bearing their baggage. Striking west, they started by crossing the Alleghenies, and reached a height of 3,000 feet before descending. They later reached the upper Youghiogheny some thirty-five miles from Wills Creek and from there struck north-west and climbed the 2,400-feet Laurel Ridge to reach the plateau some 1,700 feet above sea level[1] lying beyond and stretching towards Chestnut Ridge to the north. Gist had named the plateau Great Meadows, and it interested Washington because although somewhat boggy in places it had fewer thickets than the country they had so far crossed, and seemed more suitable for settlement. On Sunday, 18 November, having travelled seventy miles from Wills Creek and crossed Chestnut Ridge, they reached Gist's settlement, after which they moved over to the right bank of the Youghiogheny, followed the river north to its junction with the Monongahela, and then went on towards Turtle Creek where Frazier's store was situated.

The trader had much to tell them. Friendly natives headed by Half King had recently visited him, he said, and had left a string of wampum and a message for the Lieutenant-Governor of Virginia saying that France's Indian allies had taken up the hatchet against the English. However, General de Marin, the French commandor, had recently died and the greater part of the French forces had temporarily withdrawn northward to winter quarters, so that the area was relatively quiet at the moment.

From Frazier's, Washington's party passed east of the Ohio Forks where the turbulent Allegheny meets the slower-flowing waters of the Monongahela. There, or nearby, Governor Dinwiddie had planned to erect his fort. Trent was considering building it north of the Ohio on the route to Logstown, but Washington thought the land between the rivers offered a better position; and that is where it was set up.

The men and baggage were taken across the Allegheny in canoes while the horses were persuaded to swim the chilly stream, and on reaching the other side the party found themselves on the north bank of the Ohio down which they could ride to their first objective, the huts and longhouse known as Logstown. This was the scene of many Indian conferences, and where Washington was to meet Half King.

Half King, who was the most important sachem of the area, was then

[1] As a trained surveyor Washington made careful note of heights and distances.

about fifty-three years old. A loyal friend of the English, he expressed to Washington resentment at the treatment he had recently received at the hands of the now defunct General de Marin. When Washington enquired about the best routes to the nearest French fort, and asked if he could provide an escort, the chief not only agreed to do so but said he would accompany the party to make his own complaint to the French. He said he

Washington as a surveyor

would tell the new commandant what he had said to de Marin, namely, 'This is our land, not yours. If you had come in a peaceable manner like our brothers the English we should not be against your trading with us as they do; but to come, fathers, and build houses on our land and take it by force is what we cannot submit to.'

General de Marin had replied contemptuously, saying, according to Half King: 'I am not afraid of flies or mosquitoes, and Indians are such as these. I tell you down that river I will go and will build upon it according to my command. If the river was blocked up I have forces sufficient to burst it open and tread under my feet all that stand in opposition together with their alliances, for my force is as the sand of the seashore. Therefore, here is your wampum! I fling it at you!'

After a short delay while the sachems discussed the size of the escort they could provide, Washington's party set out. Following an uneventful march of some fifty miles, on approaching Venango they saw to their chagrin the fleur-de-lys already flying above the trading post. The commander Captain Philippe Joncaire, whose mother was a Seneca squaw, received them with the utmost courtesy; but he refused to accept Dinwiddie's letter of complaint, and referred them to his superior at Le Boeuf in the north.

While at Venango, Joncaire, who was understandably one of the shrewdest of the French in dealing with Indians, started to use his wiles on Half King, directly the latter announced he intended to deliver back the wampum belt of friendship and warn the French to leave his land. The Frenchman acted as if the Indians with Washington were the closest of allies and warmest of friends. He gave them presents and plied them with brandy. Eventually he made them so drunk that not only was there no question of telling the French to quit, but Washington found it extremely difficult to persuade the Indians to leave Venango at all.

At Le Boeuf, Washington was received by a Captain St. Pierre[1] to whom he presented his letter and asked for an early reply. While the French officers were perusing it, Washington and his companions had time to examine the fort and stockade, to note the nature of the armaments, and to count the number of war canoes in the creek. When he had read the letter St. Pierre suggested that Washington should go on to Quebec to present it to the Governor-General of Canada. This Washington flatly declined to do. He said his orders were to deliver the letter to the commander on the frontier the French had occupied. St. Pierre then agreed to draft a reply; and Washington, having urged Half King to seek an audience to return the treaty belt and make his speech of complaint, planned to leave next day. However, the French at Le Boeuf adopted the same attitude towards the Indians as those at Venango. When Half King came back to Washington he had a lame tale to tell. He had undertaken to

[1] Full title: Sieur Legardeur de St. Pierre de Repentigny.

deliver back the wampum; but St. Pierre had been unwilling to accept it. The Frenchman protested that he had great friendship for the Indians over whom Half King held sway. The French wished to trade with the tribes, he said, and as proof of this, would send goods immediately to Logstown. Washington had already heard that some of the French were going downstream. Coupled with what had previously been said about seizing English traders on the Ohio, St. Pierre's talk of forwarding goods to Logstown made him suspect that the French were moving south to pick up traders. In any case his hosts were ready to speed their parting guests. That very evening a written answer was received to Governor Dinwiddie's letter. Along with the paper was an assurance that canoes laden with provisions would be at Washington's disposal next morning.

But Washington still had the problem of persuading the Indians to accompany him on the return journey. Every blandishment was being offered to keep them from leaving. There were hints of much pleasure for Half King and his companions if they remained. It was not cleverly done. The artifice was plain; but defeating it was another matter. Washington said afterwards: 'I can't say that ever in my life I suffered so much anxiety as I did in this affair. I saw that every stratagem which the most fruitful brain could invent was being practised to win Half King to their interest, and that leaving him behind would give them the opportunity they aimed at.'[1] Washington realised that this was a critical affair on which the continued support of the Six Nations[2] for the English cause might depend. He went straight to Half King and with all the strength of argument at his command tried to prevail on the chief to depart with him. Eventually he succeeded. The Indians reluctantly agreed to accompany the Virginians on their return to Logstown.

*

Winter had now set in, and on almost every day they had to endure rain or snow. Eager to get the French reply back as soon as possible, Washington and Gist left the rest of the party with the worn-out horses and went forward on foot to Frazier's to acquire fresh mounts. After narrowly escaping being murdered by their sole Indian guide, they next were marooned on an island while trying to cross the Allegheny on an improvised raft. However, after spending a miserably cold night, they woke to find that the frost had frozen the river solid from the shore of their island to the bank that was their goal. Crossing without any sort of trouble, they

---

[1] G. W. Writings I, Fort 33.

[2] The Iroquois confederacy which included the Seneca Mingos.

then walked ten miles and arrived at the hospitable door of John Frazier's cabin. The remaining days of the mission were tedious, but not dangerous. With fresh horses they made their way back in something like comfort, and arrived at Williamsburg precisely one month after they had left Le Boeuf—the season considered, a splendid achievement.

*

Washington's first expedition had brought him in touch with the French. His second, however, was to give him the opportunity of actually fighting them, for on the receipt of the French reply, which was a courteous but firm refusal to recognise the English claim, Dinwiddie decided to use force to try to halt the French advance.

After an unsuccessful attempt to raise militia for the task, Dinwiddie set about enlisting volunteers, enticing them with offers of shares in 200,000 transmontane acres in addition to the regulation daily pay of fifteen pounds of tobacco allowed an infantryman. Command of the force was given to Colonel Joshua Fry, a militia officer with frontier experience, and Washington, for whom a generous offer of acres was a strong allure, applied to serve and was appointed second-in-command.

Washington and Gist crossing the Allegheny

Washington was first given the task of taking the leading companies of the expedition to the advanced base at Wills Creek. When he arrived there he was met by Trent's men who he found had been driven away from the Ohio Forks by the French. They had much to tell him. Apparently, following Washington's recommendation, the fort had been constructed between the rivers; but it had hardly been completed before a large force of French arrived on the scene in canoes. Trent was away. Only his brother-in-law Edward Ward, some forty soldiers, Half King and a few Indians were available to defend the post. When the French commander told Ward he had an hour to decide whether to surrender or face bombardment, Half King, remembering Joncaire's tactics of the previous winter, told Ward to say he had not the authority to comply with such a demand and must refer it to Trent. But the French would have none of that. Ward must surrender instantly. If he did so he and his men could leave unharmed with their tools and belongings.

As Ward estimated that the French outnumbered him ten times, he decided to accept their terms. Thus, he and Half King marched out. The chief was still defiant. He shouted out as he passed the French that he had ordered the fort to be built and laid the first log.[1]

*

Spurred on by the news that the French were on the move again, Washington, taking his baggage and swivel-guns, advanced from Wills Creek, crossed the Alleghenies and, following the route of the previous winter, reached Great Meadows where he encamped in an open glade by a running brook assuring a water supply near the junction of Great Meadows Run and Indian Run, whose banks provided natural entrenchments. The day after he set up camp, Christopher Gist rode in, and after greeting his companion of the mission to Le Boeuf, described how the French had just raided his settlement, killed his cow and threatened to destroy all his belongings. When Gist told him the French had left their canoes at Redstone Creek, Washington realised they were far from their base and might well be cut off. He was further encouraged to attempt an ambush when joined next day by Half King and forty Indian followers who were skilled in such affairs. Indian scouts were sent out, and these soon returned to report that the small French force was in hiding in a glen on Chestnut Ridge. Next, the English and their Indian allies advanced silently through the woods and fell on their adversaries. Although caught by surprise in

[1] The French later built a stronger fort on the same site and named it Fort Duquesne after the Marquis Duquesne, Governor-General of Canada 1752–55.

their hiding place, the French managed to spring to arms, but they were so outnumbered, they could not accomplish very much. When their leader Captain Jumonville was killed they gave ground and made off. Then most of them came running back. They had found Washington's Indians in the rear, and knowing their likely fate at the Mingos' hands had quickly decided to return and surrender to the English. Behind the French came Half-King's warriors, braining and scalping the laggard wounded they found in their path. They wanted the unwounded prisoners to be handed over, to be dealt with in the same way. This Washington sternly refused to allow.

When all firing had ceased, and the twenty-one French survivors had surrendered their weapons, they were marched off under guard bound for Virginia. Left on the field of battle were ten enemy dead, including the leader, along with one wounded man who had somehow escaped the hatchet. Only one American was dead and only three wounded, so Washington's first battle had undoubtedly been a victory.

*

Although the outcome of the action on Chestnut Ridge had been decisive enough, Washington realised that a stronger enemy force might soon fall upon him seeking revenge, for, from what he now heard, the French had termed his ambush, 'an assassination of Jumonville and his men while they were on a mission of peace'. Thus, anticipating French reprisals, he sent a message to Colonel Fry at Wills Creek to ask for reinforcements. The returning messenger told Washington that Fry had been fatally injured in a fall from his horse, and that the command had devolved on Colonel Innes. However, the remainder of the Virginia Regiment, about 200 men, were sent forward and arrived on 9 June, and on 12 June the South Carolina Independent Company of regular troops under Captain Mackay also reached Great Meadows.

The arrival of Captain Mackay brought up the delicate subject of regulars ranking provincials, for it was not certain whether Washington could give orders to a regular captain. Mackay made the position clear, as he saw it. When Washington sent the parole and countersign. Mackay replied that he did not think that he should receive these from a colonial colonel. Later he insisted his was a separate force and proceeded to pick his own camp site. Though he agreed to join Washington in fighting the French, he would not allow his men to help cut wagon roads or even load ammunition and stores.

*

Before moving against the main French force, which he now learnt was approaching, Washington sent off messengers to seek more Indian aid from a friendly sachem near Logstown. Having done this, he marched his 300 men north to Gist's settlement, planning to meet his new allies at Redstone Creek to the west. From Gist's he had just despatched a body of men to cut a wagon road to Redstone when he received news that a French force was close at hand. Abandoning the idea of consolidating at Redstone Creek, he called back the road builders, marched his men south, and assembled his entire command, including Mackay's men, at his previous camp at Great Meadows. This was already partially entrenched; but he proceeded to improve its defences. 'The whole and the parts were not a design of engineering but of frontier necessity,' he was later to write, 'so I gave it the name Fort Necessity.'

After Washington and his men were installed, a force of 500 French with as many Indians arrived on the scene. These proceeded to surround the compound and open fire on the defenders. Before the encirclement was completed, Washington's Indian allies, including the usually loyal Half King, mistrusting the English chances of success, slipped silently away. Although Washington had managed to strengthen the fortifications of his camp during the respite before the French approach, the chances of holding out against such a large enemy force were so slight that after a token resistance he agreed to parley. The terms finally agreed on declared that two officer hostages were to be left with the French as a guarantee for the return of the prisoners taken in the earlier engagement, but with this proviso, Washington was permitted to march out his men unmolested and take them back to Virginia. However, in the second fight on the Ohio at the start of the French and Indian War[1] the French definitely had the advantage.

*

Washington's enforced surrender at Fort Necessity did not deter him from taking part in further military adventures, and when in 1754 General Edward Braddock was ordered to lead a British force against the French at Fort Duquesne, he immediately sought permission to join the column and was appointed to be one of Braddock's aides.

Braddock led his force at a slow pace along the route Washington had previously followed to Gist's Plantation, after which he continued with the main body across the River Youghiogheny and marched on towards the Forks, while his second-in-command, Colonel Dunbar, set up a base

[1] The name for the American theatre of the Seven Years War 1756–63.

camp short of the river. To avoid the scrub and marsh in the neighbourhood of Turtle Creek the head of the column crossed back over the
River Monongahela and followed its west bank across the great bend
before recrossing a few miles from Fort Duquesne. Colonel Gage[1] with an
advance party and two six-pounders led the way over, and having blazed
a trail across the bend, took up a position on the far bank on the way to
Fort Duquesne to cover the crossing of the rest of the army. Then followed Colonel St. Clair, Braddock's quartermaster, with pioneers who
cut inclines down the banks of the river at both fording places. These
operations and the crosssing by the army were carried out extremely
smoothly. It was said that Braddock would not have been ashamed to have
organised such a march in Flanders, or to have made it even while His

Washington's pistol

Royal Highness the Duke of Cumberland was present. The same professional skill was shown when the whole force was over the river and on
its way to Fort Duquesne. Gage was in the van again, followed by engineers who marked the route by striking the bark off the trees to be felled to
provide a twelve-foot roadway. This was considered wide enough for the
guns and wagons. The men could look after themselves. By the time the
force cleared the curve in the trail by Frazier's post all were in high spirits.
It had been thought that the only place where the advance of the column
was likely to be disputed was at the fords. Now everyone was across, it
was believed the rest of the campaign would be easy.

Braddock and his aides halfway down the column were equally relieved that the crossing had been made without interference. Washington
had played no part in the approach march. Smitten with fever he had

[1] Later Gage was to command the British troops at Boston at the start of the American
Revolutionary War.

been nearly jolted to death riding in a wagon; though he had been lucky to find one, for he had tried to persuade Braddock to use pack animals. Now, though still weak, he was back in the saddle at Braddock's side.

*

The French at Fort Duquesne had received reports from their scouts that the British had reached Turtle Creek and were turning to cross the Monongahela; and they immediately realised that the best time to attack was when the British were passing over the river. However, there was a delay while sufficient Indians were being persuaded to take part; and by the time 250 French and Canadians and 650 Indians had been assembled, the British had completed their two crossings. As a second best the French decided to stage an ambush on the column while it was snaking through the forest; and they found a good place to carry it out where there were ravines to provide cover and a hill from which to pour down a deadly fire.

The British had advanced less than a mile from the second ford when there came the sound of firing from the front, the roll of a volley, and then scattered fire followed by another volley. Although they had scouts out the enemy's appearance was quite unexpected. Surprise was complete. Yet when the French attacked, swarming through the trees, the Indians whooping and shrieking, the British van held their ground and fired a volley which brought down the enemy commander mortally wounded and caused some Canadians to flee the field. However, the French soon rallied. Making use of the ample cover they began picking off the redcoats who could now do no more than fire aimlessly and ineffectively at unseen foes. As the firing moved down on both sides of the column, and started to come from a hill on the right, rumours spread that the baggage train was being attacked. This proved too much for the stunned soldiery of the van. Believing they were going to be surrounded, they fled in disorder to the rear, leaving two guns in enemy hands, bumping into men from the main body, and passing on their own confusion to their comrades.

Braddock now rode up with his aides. He found several abject groups of redcoats bunched on the track through the woods stubbornly refusing to obey orders to counter-attack. Appreciating the situation, he instructed his aides to try and rally parties to recapture the guns and storm the hill. Washington then took a hand. He persuaded Captain Waggoner, a veteran of Fort Necessity, to make an attempt on the hill; and the latter led some men up the slope to a fallen tree from which the enemy sharp-

General Edward Braddock

shooters were in view. Crouching by the tree, however, they came under fire from their own people, and they had to be withdrawn. Next, Colonel Burton led some of the 48th part of the way to the crest. They too could not maintain their position. Other officers also tried to rally men to counter-attack; but the only one to achieve anything was a colonial officer who broke up an enemy attack by posting his men Indian fashion behind trees.

In despair Braddock ordered a retirement on the baggage wagons. These provided nothing of a rallying point. The waggoners cut loose their horses, mounted, and made off for the ford; and they were soon followed by a mob of frightened soldiers. Braddock while trying to rally his men had five horses shot under him. Then he was struck himself in the right arm and lung. Washington who had lost two horses now realised that all was lost, and the first task he set himself was to get the general away from the battlefield. Finding a cart for Braddock, he collected an escort and set off on the road for home. After crossing the first ford he planned to set up a defended position in the bend of the river and await reinforcements from the base camps, but sufficient men could not be gathered to man the defences, and the retreat was continued. After recrossing the Monongahela Washington went ahead on the long stretch to the Youghiogheny ford and base camp with a message to Dunbar to send reinforcements. After a gruelling ride he reached the camp, but found it in great confusion following the news of the defeat of the main body. Dunbar's men were so fearful of sharing the fate of their comrades that their commander was unable to raise a force to march against the enemy; but he did manage to send forward some wagons bearing provisions for the routed army.

A few days later the main group of survivors along with the stricken Braddock arrived at the base, and with his approval large quantities of wagons, guns and shot and shell were destroyed or buried. Then, the next day, they all left on the long march home. Just short of Fort Necessity, the scene of Washington's earlier defeat, Braddock called a halt. He realised he was no longer well enough to direct the retreat, so called Dunbar to him and in a few words turned over the command. It is said that he also exclaimed, as if to himself: 'We shall better know how to deal with them another time.' When the ragged column had gone only a few miles farther, Braddock halted it again. This time he called Lieutenant Orme, his favourite aide, and directed him to send a message to headquarters explaining what had happened and pointing out that 'nothing could equal the gallantry and good conduct of the officers nor the bad behaviour of the men'. Then, according to his aide, 'in that pride of his corps and with that shame of his troops the general died'.[1]

Washington was charged with the responsibility of the burial. He had a deep grave dug in the middle of the trail, and when the body had been interred, ordered the wagons to pass over and the troops to tramp down the earth so that the Indians would not be able to discover the spot. After which they set off on the last stage of the journey to Fort Cumberland and home, Washington having received a lesson in how not to conduct an operation; but somewhat comforted by the way the colonials had behaved.

*

After his return, Washington, although only twenty-three, was appointed commander of Virginia's frontier force and assigned the task of defending her western border. He was beset with difficulties during these operations, for there was an almost total lack of regular supplies and his defence force was repeatedly depleted because of short enlistments, deser-

[1] Orme 357.

tion and the non-appearance of replacements. However, he tackled the task in a painstaking way and gained valuable experience thereby.

In 1758, his job on the frontier done, but still thirsting for military adventure, Washington went on yet another expedition against Fort Duquesne. During this operation he might very well have gained more valuable experience, for both Brigadier General Forbes, the commander, and his deputy Bouquet were first-rate leaders; but he put himself at a disadvantage by obstinately insisting that Braddock's route to the Ohio was better than the northern route Forbes chose; and in any case there was not much fighting done. Forbes moved forward slowly and methodically and, unlike Braddock who had only one base, he set up a whole series as he advanced, so that there was little danger of his being surprised far out in the wilds with no reinforcements nearby. Forbes unwisely allowed a detachment under Major Grant to attempt a night attack on Fort Duquesne but, after this had not unexpectedly failed, he made no more mistakes. In fact, he gained his objective without further bloodshed, for the French burned and abandoned the fortress before a shot had been fired. There had been no battle, no flags, no booty, no surrendered arms; but Forbes like a good soldier was well content, for he had made a great conquest at small loss of life.

*

After the expedition to Fort Duquesne Washington resigned his com-

Mount Vernon by William Birch

mission and married Martha, née Dandridge, the rich widow of Daniel Parke Custis. For the next sixteen years from 1759 to 1775 he lived at the Washington family home of Mount Vernon beside the Potomac and looked after his own and his wife's plantations, successfully growing tobacco, flax and wheat, and also carrying out milling operations and fishing commercially in the nearby estuary. Before long he was made a burgess and became involved in the government of the colony; and he also voluntarily took charge of the financial affairs of members of his own family and of several of his neighbours. A busier man it would have been hard to find in the whole of North America; but although it is a wonder he found time to carry out all he set himself to do, there is no doubt that this period prepared him in some degree for the onerous tasks he was given in the coming conflict, whose first rumblings were heard while he was at Mount Vernon.

*

In 1764 England's pride in the victorious close of the Seven Years War was tempered by the realisation of the huge debt it had brought in its train and the consequent necessity for high taxation. Worse, the prospect of additional expense had to be faced in order to defend the new-won empire, for in North America alone it was planned to keep a force of 6,000 men.

It did not take long for the authorities to decide that the colonists would have to contribute towards the cost of their own defence, and in 1764 a tax of threepence a gallon was imposed on molasses imported into America from the West Indies to raise funds for this purpose.

Colonial opposition was immediate and vociferous, and loudest from the people of the port of Boston who were most affected. Here the arch rebel Samuel Adams evolved the theory that the British had not the right to impose taxation on Americans because the latter had no representatives in the home government. His utterance 'No Taxation without Representation' was to become the battle cry of the rebellion.

About this time it was being mooted by the home government that a stamp tax might be the best way of providing the necessary revenue for defence purposes; and the details of what such a tax might entail were brought to the notice of the colonial assemblies.

Even the prior notice of this impost brought forth strong protests; and in March 1765, after the Stamp Act had been introduced, the young lawyer Patrick Henry laid before the Virginia House of Burgesses a series of resolutions delineating the colonists' traditional rights and privileges. Following the same line of argument as Samuel Adams, Henry endeavoured to show that the only taxes permissible were ones imposed by the colonists themselves.

The Virginia Resolves along with similar protests in other colonies made a tremendous impact on the country. There was widespread mob violence, stamp agents were forced to resign, and in Boston so-called Sons of Liberty burned the records of the vice-admiralty court and looted the homes of officials.

Such was the turmoil, that delegates from the colonies met in New York to consider what should be done; and as a result of this meeting a despatch was sent to England demanding the repeal of the Stamp Act.

Next, to exert additional pressure on the home government, the leading merchants of Boston, New York and Philadelphia entered into a non-importation agreement whereby no goods would be bought from England while the Stamp Act remained on the Statute Book.

*

After two months of heated debate in the English Parliament the Stamp Act was repealed, mainly due to the influence of William Pitt. But this was by no means the end of the matter. The British were still intent on making the colonists pay for their own defence; and in 1767 Townsend introduced for the purpose imposts on glass, lead, paints, paper and tea entering America. It was soon, however, to become abundantly clear that the colonists were opposed to taxation whatever its form, for protests against the new taxes became, over the years, as violent as those against the Stamp Act had been.

An early confrontation does not appear to have been directly due to the new taxation. During a street brawl on 5 March 1770, British soldiers on sentry duty, having been harried by rioters, opened fire and killed six Americans. The incident soon came to be called 'The Boston Massacre', and was widely used thereafter by the colonists for propaganda purposes to illustrate how severely they were being oppressed.

In June 1772 there was a noteworthy protest against taxation when the British customs schooner *Gaspée* was burnt to the water line as she lay grounded near Providence.

Then, in December 1773, all the Townsend Taxes having been withdrawn except the one on tea, protesters disguised as Indians stormed tea ships in Boston harbour and dumped 342 chests in the water.

King George III had insisted on the retention of the tea tax as a token of the royal rights to tax, and on hearing of this last outrage demanded the punishment of the offenders. Consequently, in June 1774, was passed the

The Boston Massacre, 5 March 1770, engraving by Paul Revere (courtesy of the Metropolitan Museum of Art, gift of Mrs. Russell Sage, 1910)

Boston Port Act which closed the harbour to all traffic until such time as the losses caused by the 'Boston Tea Party' has been made good. To enforce the Port Act a substantial body of troops was despatched to reinforce the garrison at Boston. Finally General Gage was appointed Governor of Massachusetts with instructions to try and nip the incipient rebellion in the bud. Thus the stage was set for the coming conflict.

*

When the news of the Boston Port Act reached Virginia it did not at first produce much effect, for the merchants there were not as numerous or as influential as those in Massachusetts. Later, however, when it came to be seen as another severe infringement of colonists' liberties, protest action was taken in Virginia, including a new non-importation agreement and the threat of a non-exportation measure.

Washington had not so far been greatly concerned in the quarrel with England. He was not anxious to participate in a non-exportation measure as he had tobacco he wanted to sell; but he appears to have supported another non-importation agreement, for he writes on 20 July 1774 to Bryan Fairfax: 'I think, at least I hope, that there is enough public virtue left among us to deny ourselves everything but the bare necessities of life to accomplish this end.'

From this time onwards Washington willy-nilly became very much more involved, for his position as a burgess was to bring him into the very centre of affairs. In August 1774 a convention was held in the House of Burgesses at Williamsburg where it was agreed to send seven delegates to a Continental Congress at Philadelphia. These delegates, who included Washington, took with them a resolution stating that the importation of British goods should be immediately halted, and that unless American grievances were redressed the exportation of American products to Britain should also be stopped.

At this first meeting, at which all the colonies except Georgia were represented, delegates drifted in, deliberations were slow to start, and proceedings were conducted in so ponderous a manner, and meandered so much, that on leaving few were clear on what exactly had been decided. However, a non-importation had undoubtedly been endorsed, and, it seemed, non-exportation was being threatened should the Boston Port Act not be soon repealed.

*

A year later another and more business-like congress was called at Philadelphia, and Washington again was one of the delegates from Virginia.

By this time the skirmishes at Lexington and Concord[1] had taken place and 'the shot that rang round the world' had been fired, so that the delegates had more specific matters to consider, including the raising of fighting men to support the New Englanders already engaged and the selection of a commander-in-chief of the colonial armies.

On 14 May 1775 Washington was present at a discussion on the number and type of troops to be embodied, and after this subject had been deliberated at length, John Adams from Massachusetts rose and pleaded that the forces be raised quickly, for if the New Englanders before Boston were not reinforced soon, they might very well dissolve, and then the task of raising another local force would be extremely difficult. He went on to stress the need also for the early appointment of a commander-in-chief responsible to Congress. Washington then heard Adams say that although the choice of a leader was not easy he had someone in mind; on which John Hancock, also from Massachusetts and in the chair, showed manifest pleasure as if he were certain Adams was about to call his name. Washington, meanwhile, fearing otherwise, felt embarrassment creep over him. Adams did not prolong the suspense. The commander he had in mind, he said, was a gentleman from Virginia. On the instant John Hancock's expression changed; his disappointment was beyond concealment, the tightening of his lips and the flash of his eye showed he felt that Adams had betrayed his expectations. Adams observed this but went straight on. He referred, he said, to one whose skill and experience as an officer, whose independent fortune . . . with that Washington bolted towards the adjoining library, for Adams could be talking of no other than him.

[1] See pp 22–40.

John Hancock by John Singleton Copley (Courtesy, Museum of Fine Arts, Boston)

The debate ended without any decision being made, though now Washington's name had been mentioned, his friends did not hesitate to seek support for him. Southerners who had deferred to New Englanders needed to hear no other argument than that he was acceptable to Massachusetts and Connecticut. Men from the latter colonies accepted that his election was expedient in order to assure full Southern support in the struggle against the British. No one at the outset showed any disposition to attribute to him any great military qualities, but all appeared to admire him for his rectitude, sound judgment and business experience. Eliphalet Dyer probably spoke the mind of many when he announced that Washington was highly esteemed by those who knew him, but 'as to military and real service he knows no more than some of ours'. In the end expediency to assure full Southern support seems to have prevailed even though the impression of Washington's martial ability had failed to convince that he was preeminently the man to head the army. In any case within a few hours after Adams spoke, all opposition to Washington evaporated and by Thursday 15 June 1775, when the discussion was resumed, everything pointed to his selection.

Having stayed away from the assembly, Washington knew nothing of the deliberations until he met the delegates leaving the hall about dinner time on the last day. The delegates shook him by the hand, congratulated him, and said that at the end of the debate it had been resolved 'that a general be appointed to command all the Continental forces raised for the defence of liberty', and, after his name had been proposed, no other being put forward his election was unanimous.

*

Washington was called next day to the State House. There John Hancock, who by this time had recovered from the disappointment over failure to receive the command, good-humouredly announced that Washington had been chosen by Congress to be their commander-in-chief. On this, Washington rose and bowed to the chair. Then he drew a paper from his pocket and read out solemnly his formal acceptance, saying that he was deeply honoured, felt distressed at his inadequacy for the task, but pledged he would do his very best to promote the 'glorious cause'.

Thus, although Washington did not consider himself sufficiently experienced for such a responsible post, the urge to serve his country—like the urge in the past to serve Virginia and win thereby the approbation of his fellows—seems to have compelled him to accept. He was to say later that it was as if Divine Providence had directed him to take on the grave responsibility of commanding the colonial forces.

Chapter Two

LEXINGTON AND CONCORD

'The shot that rang round the world.'

At the Colonial Congress in Philadelphia when non-exportation and non-importation agreements were drawn up to put pressure on the British government to redress American grievances, it was also suggested that rebel provincial congresses should establish full-time Committees of Safety to ensure that these agreements were honoured. The Committees were duly formed and took upon themselves additional tasks, such as pressing loyalists to join the rebel cause and mustering resources for a possible armed conflict with the authorities.

Massachusetts, who led the way, had thirty militia regiments most of whose members had weapons of sorts left over from the French and Indian War. But command lay in Tory hands, so the Committee sent out orders that all militia officers must resign. The Patriots did so willingly; the Loyalists under intimidation followed suit. Then, new officers were elected, all favouring the rebel cause.

After this it was directed that each company of militia should enlist a fourth of its men 'to act on a minute's notice'—and so came into being the famous 'Minutemen' of the American Revolutionary War. Finally, Artemas Ward, a veteran of the French and Indian War, was chosen as commanding officer of all the militia, and the collection of arms and ammunition was begun under the direction of the Committee of Safety. Small arms and ammunition were purchased, and with firelocks stolen from Gage's soldiers and cannon seized from outlying British works, a considerable quantity of warlike stones was collected, the bulk being stored at Worcester and Concord.

Connecticut, Rhode Island and New Hampshire were soon to follow the example of Massachusetts, and by mid-December 1774 militiamen in possession of weapons and ammunition were drilling on village commons throughout New England.

*

In February 1775 an attempt was made at reconciliation when Lord North offered a policy of forbearance if the colonies would tax themselves. But restrictions on trade were to remain and there were limitations for the Americans in fishing on the Newfoundland Banks. These restrictions were not acceptable to the colonists who depended so much on the sea for their living, and the result was that they continued to prepare for war. When it became clear that the colonists were bent on confrontation, instructions were sent to General Gage from London telling him to try and quell the rebellion.

*

Inside Boston an uneasy peace existed between the British troops and the populace. To start with, the local inhabitants had been placatory, trying to persuade the soldiers to desert. Then they began to abuse the redcoats, or set on them in mobs as had happened during the Boston Massacre of 1770. They also managed to persuade a number of soldiers to sell their firelocks which were all too easily conveyed out of the town without being discovered by the guards.

At times there was a situation approaching a rebellion within the town. For example, on 6 March 1775—5 March being a Sunday—John Hancock, John Adams and his cousin Samuel Adams were bold enough to organise an oration in the principal church, commemorating the Boston Massacre of 1770.

Lieutenant Mackenzie of the 23rd Regiment of Foot records that when Dr. Joseph Warren ascended the pulpit to deliver it, 'every person was silent and every countenance seemed to denote that some event of consequence might be expected'. The oration though severe on the conduct of the military, and calculated to excite resentment, was delivered without interruption except for some hisses from some officers present. When it ended Samuel Adams rose from a pew near the pulpit and moved that 'another oration should be delivered on 5 March next to commemorate the bloody massacre of 5 March 1770'. On this, several officers began to cry out, 'Oh fie! Oh fie!' and a great bustle ensued. As everyone was now on the move, intending to go out, there was a considerable amount of noise and the officers' words were mistaken for 'Fire! Fire!' Then someone actually called out 'Fire!' which created a scene of the greatest confusion imaginable. There were a number of women present and their cries intensified the confusion, which was further increased by the drums and

Samuel Adams by John Singleton Copley (Courtesy, Museum of Fine Arts, Boston)

fifes of the 43rd Regiment which happened to be passing from exercise. People started leaping out of the lower windows and in a short time the meeting was nearly cleared. As soon as the mistake was discovered and the atmosphere grew quiet, the leaders proceeded to the choice of public officers, which being finished, the people dispersed. Mackenzie concludes: 'Some of the leaders were extremely alarmed when they heard the drums of the 43rd Regiment, as it is supposed they expected to be apprehended. The townspeople certainly expected a riot as almost every man had a short stick or bludgeon in his hand. They no doubt supposed that something said in the oration would have induced the officers to act improperly and strike or lay hands on some of the party, which would have been the signal for battle. It is certain that both sides were ripe for it and a single blow would have occasioned the commencement of hostilities. Fortunately nothing of the kind happened nor was any person hurt in the confusion.'

*

General Gage had established a comprehensive network of spies to discover what was happening in the country areas across the water from Boston, and he had supplemented the information he received by sending out patrols of officers and columns of troops on marches through the countryside. Thus, on receipt of his orders to deal with the rebellion, he decided to send a column to destroy the cannon and warlike stores which he had learnt were being assembled by militant colonists at Concord. To command this expedition he chose Colonel Smith of the 10th Regiment; and the order[1] he gave to that officer explains clearly what he wanted done:

Boston, April 18, 1775

Lieut. Colonel Smith, 10th Regiment Foot.
Sir,

Having received intelligence that a quantity of Ammunition, Provision, Artillery, Tents and small arms, have been collected at Concord, for the Avowed Purpose of raising and supporting a Rebellion against His Majesty, you will march the Corps of Grenadiers and Light Infantry, under your Command, with the utmost expedition and Secrecy to Concord, where you will seize and destroy all Artillery, Ammunition, Provisions, Tents, Small Arms, and all Military Stores whatever. But you will take care the soldiers do not plunder the inhabitants, or hurt private property.

You have a Draught (map) of Concord, on which is marked the Houses, Barns etc. which contain the above military stores. You will order a Trunnion to be knocked off each gun, but if it is found impracticable on any, they must be spiked, and the Carriages destroyed. The Powder and flower (flour) must be shook out of the Barrels into the River, the Tents burned, Pork or Beef destroyed in the best way you can devise. And the men may put balls of lead in their pockaps, throwing them by degrees in Ponds, Ditches etc. but no quantity together so that they may be recovered afterwards.

If you meet any Brass Artillery, you will order their muzzles to be beat in so as to render them useless.

You will observe by the Draught that it will be necessary to secure the two Bridges as soon as possible, you will therefore order a party of the best Marchers to go on with expedition for the purpose.

A small party on Horseback is ordered out to stop all advice of your March getting to Concord before you, and a small number of Artillery (artillerymen) go out in Chaises to wait for you on the road, with Sledge Hammers, Spikes etc.

You will open your business and return with the Troops as soon as possible, which I must leave to your own Judgement and Discretion. I am, Sir,
Your most obedient humble servant.
Thos. Gage

Although the preparations for the expedition were made as secretly as possible the design soon became known in Boston. The silversmith-dentist and express rider Paul Revere was the first to become suspicious when he noticed that the grenadier and light companies of the British regiments stationed in Boston had been taken off normal duties; and he reported the fact to Dr. Joseph Warren, Boston's liaison man with the

[1] Gage manuscripts.

General Thomas Gage by David Martin

local Committee of Safety.

The whole Provincial Congress had recently met defiantly in Concord, and although most of its members had left, John Hancock and Samuel Adams, who had both attended, were staying with the Rev. Jonas Clarke at Lexington. Therefore, when he received Revere's warning, one of Dr. Warren's first actions was to warn the Committee of Safety of the likelihood of a British operation in the neighbourhood. The Committee in its turn dispatched some minutemen to guard the Clarke house, and it also ordered that some of the cannon in Concord should be transferred to Groton and other safer adjacent towns.

After this, a signalling system was set up to let the countryside know the route the British were taking. Two lighted lanterns were to be hung on the steeple of North Church, Boston, if the British appeared to be coming in boats across the River Charles; one lantern if they were going on foot by Boston Neck in the south.

Later that night when British troops were seen embarking at Back Bay, and it became obvious that the water route was going to be used, the two lanterns were duly hoisted. But, not content with this, Dr. Warren also sent off Paul Revere and his fellow express rider William Dawes to give warning to the countryside.

Revere was taken across in a rowing boat from the ferry by two friends using muffled oars. On arrival in Charlestown he borrowed a horse from Deacon Larkin and rode off. He started towards Cambridge, but just short of Prospect Hill ran into the mounted patrol Gage had sent out in advance of the column, to stop anyone attempting to alert the countryside. Wheeling round, Revere set spurs to his horse and quickly outdistanced his pursuers. He took the road north to Medford, and from there turned west to Menotomy (now Arlington) which he reached without hindrance. He arrived at Lexington just as the church clock was striking midnight and rode up to the Clarke home to warn the two provincial congressmen who were staying there. The minutemen outside the Rev. Mr. Clarke's house would not at first let the express rider pass. They said the family did not wish to be disturbed by any noise. 'Noise!' Revere cried out angrily. 'You'll have noise enough before long. The Regulars are coming out!'

Once Revere had been allowed to go into the house he found Hancock and Adams sitting together drinking tea in the front hall, and after telling them about the British column, begged them to leave before the troops arrived.

Paul Revere by John Singleton Copley (Courtesy, Museum of Fine Arts, Boston)

The pugnacious Hancock declared he would rather stay and fight it out. But Adams placed a hand on his shoulder and exclaimed: 'We are for the cabinet, you and I, not for the field of battle,' after which Hancock agreed to leave.

Meanwhile Dawes had managed to elude the sentries on Boston Neck and had passed through Roxbury and Cambridge without hindrance. He arrived at Lexington about half an hour after Revere. Between the two of them they managed to rouse most of the town. After which they started off together to do the same in Lincoln and Concord.

Just short of Lincoln the two express riders were caught up by Dr. Samuel Prescott who had been visiting his sweetheart in Lexington. They were riding along unconcerned, Revere in front and Dawes and Prescott a little way behind, when they were suddenly apprehended by the same British mounted patrol that had earlier accosted Revere.

Dawes, with considerable presence of mind, turned his horse quickly and sped safely down the road back to Lexington. Prescott too managed to escape. He jumped his horse over the stone wall ahead, made his way down a farm track by a swamp, and was able to carry the alarm to Lincoln and Concord. But Revere, who was closer to the enemy and therefore at a disadvantage, could only make for the wood at the foot of the pasture they were crossing. He was quickly overtaken, and his famous ride was ended, for the enemy grabbed his bridle, put pistols to his breast and forced him to dismount.

*

On Lexington Green, soon after Revere's arrival with the news of the march of the British column, the bell in the wooden belfry between the meeting house and the school was set ringing to give the alarm. The sound soon brought the Lexington minutemen to the Green; but when their leader Captain John Parker realised the British must be still a long way off, he dismissed them with instructions to assemble again later directly they heard the beat of the drum. Those who lived nearby went home. The rest repaired to the Buckman Tavern on the east of the Green where, after placing their muskets in the rack on the wall, they settled down to drink flip and smoke clay pipes beside the high bar counter,[1] while awaiting their final call to arms.

*

Meanwhile, the British had made slow progress. According to the

---

[1] The Tavern has been furnished again in period. The author was told there that if a lad was tall enough to see over its counter he could buy a drink.

account of an officer with the van,[1] they left Boston at 10.30 p.m. on the night of 18 April 1775, but could not all be accommodated in the boats available. The boats had to leave and return several times and the start of the march on the Charlestown side was consequently much delayed. Then, on the first stage across the marshes to reach the road to Concord, the men were obliged to wade halfway up their thighs through two inlets, which was not a good start for the long march ahead. To make up time they were set off at the double-quick; but it was almost daylight before they were nearing Lexington.

As soon as news was received of the British approach, the drum was beat to assemble the minutemen on the Green. Seventy-seven appeared, which was more than the first time, and Parker lined them up in a double row across the triangle of grass between the roads.

In charge of the British van was Major Pitcairn of the Marines and when he saw the men blocking his way, he rode forward and ordered them to disperse.

Captain Parker, resolving at first to resist, cried out: 'Stand your ground! Don't fire unless fired upon! But if they mean to have a war let it

[1] An unnamed officer of the 23rd Regiment.

Minutemen on Lexington Green by W. B. Wollen

begin here!'[1]

Pitcairn, who by this time had formed the light infantry behind him into line of battle, again implored the Americans to go home; on which Parker, realising how badly he was outnumbered, ordered his men to file away. Only a few had started to go off when a single shot rang out. Who fired it has never been determined. But it decided the matter. Pitcairn immediately ordered a warning volley over the heads or the rebels; and then, when some still stood their ground aggressively, another in earnest. After which he sent in his men with the bayonet.

Though the bulk of the Americans had by this time dispersed, those who remained resisted gallantly and suffered severely, for eight were killed and nine wounded. Among those killed was Jonathan Harrington Jr, who, although mortally wounded, dragged himself to the door of his nearby home to die at his wife's feet. Jonas Parker's[2] death was even more heroic. Badly wounded, he stood his ground, and, sinking to his knees, with bullets, wadding and flints tossed in his hat at his feet, was trying to reload when a bayonet brought him down.

The British had only two soldiers wounded and Major Pitcairn's horse slashed in the flank. They considered they had won a victory. Indeed, when Colonel Smith and the main body arrived, they raised a token cheer.

*

After the whole column had formed up again, an eyewitness records: 'Several of the officers advised Colonel Smith to give up the idea of prosecuting his march and to return to Boston, as from what they had seen and the certainty of the countryside being alarmed and assembling they imagined it would be impracticable to advance to Concord and execute their orders. But Colonel Smith was determined to obey the orders he had received and accordingly pursued the march.' Indeed, to show he had been in no way put out by the encounter on Lexington Green, he set off with drums beating and the fifers playing a cheerful tune. Soon after leaving Lexington, and while still on the way to Lincoln, they met up with the patrol that had captured Revere; and Smith sent one of its members back to tell General Gage what had happened, and to ask him to dispatch Lord Percy's relief column.

By the time the British were approaching Concord, minutemen from neighbouring villages had begun to assemble. Some of these went down

[1] His famous order is engraved on the stone memorial on the Green.

[2] A cousin of Captain Parker.

the Lexington road to meet the enemy, but, when they saw how greatly they were outnumbered, they returned and formed up on a ridge beside the road. As soon as the British began to come near the minutemen left their first point of advantage and took up a new position on the hills north of the town. The ridge by the road was then occupied by British light infantry flankers who cut down the liberty pole that the rebels had erected.

On their arrival on the scene Colonel Smith and Major Pitcairn climbed to a high point in a cemetery near where the liberty pole had been and, having studied the surrounding countryside, and noted the minutemen massing on the hills north of the town, formulated the plans for carrying out their mission.

Following General Gage's instructions, three light infantry companies under Captain Laurie were sent to secure North Bridge over the Concord River; four companies under Captain Parsons were despatched to search for weapons on Colonel James Barratt's farm a mile or so beyond the bridge; and a single company was sent to secure South Bridge and search that neighbourhood.

When Colonel James Barratt, who was already under arms on the hills, saw the British making for his home he galloped back to see if the precious arms were out of sight. He had told his men to plough a pasture and hide the weapons and stores in the furrows. After he had found everything in order, he rejoined his men on the hills. Their numbers had now grown to 400, and some had started to move down towards the bridge.

Meanwhile, the grenadier companies had begun searching in the town. About 500 pounds of musket-balls were discovered and thrown into the millpond, and the Town House and Reuben's harness shop were set on fire. The latter did not burn well, however, and the inhabitants put out the flames before the dwellings were completely razed. Three iron 24-pounders were found near South Bridge and knocked off their trunnions. A quantity of flour too was destroyed. Some gun-carriages and barrels containing trenchers and wooden spoons which came to light were set on fire.

When the minutemen on the hills noticed the smoke rising, they became very alarmed. 'Are we going to let them burn down the town?' Barratt asked; and after he had received a unanimous reply demanding action, an attack on the British was organised.

This began with a march on the bridge. To the beat of the drum and with the fifes playing the 'White Cockade', a Hertford company and a

Concord company led the way. They were followed by the Acton company, three further Concord companies and the men from Bedford and Lincoln.

Meanwhile Captain Laurie, seeing the Americans approaching, and realising he was greatly outnumbered, left a few of his men to try and dismantle the bridge and withdrew the rest to the Concord side of the stream.

Directly the Americans came within range, the British opened fire, and they managed to kill the Acton leader Isaac Davis with their first volley. But they were to receive much more than they gave; and when ball after ball had smashed into them their morale went and they fled in confusion, leaving three dead and having nine wounded, four of them officers.

While retiring, strung out and in disorder, they passed on the road back to Concord the house of Elisha Jones, and Jones, who was looking out from his bedroom, could not resist trying to take pot shots at them. He got hold of his musket and pointed it through the open window; but before he could fire his Tory wife rushed in and knocked it out of his hands. Determined at least to find out what was happening, Jones then went downstairs and stood himself in the doorway of his shed to watch the redcoats pass. This was nearly his undoing, for a soldier who had noticed him earlier at the window now took a shot at him. The ball was on line but luckily for Jones flew high. However, it knocked a hole in the wall of the shed above his head—and the hole is preserved under glass in what is now called Bullet Hole House. Soon after the Jones incident the Americans who had crossed the bridge returned to the north side of the stream. Meanwhile, Colonel Smith, when he had learnt of what had been happening, ordered all his forces to assemble in the centre of Concord.

The men from South Bridge got back without incident. Directly they heard the firing in the north, they had removed the planks from the bridge to protect their retreat and after this they reached the centre of the town without harm.

Captain Parson's men who had been searching Barratt's farm recrossed the Concord River without interference and also got back safely. But they had a nasty story to tell. They had seen the bodies of two of Laurie's men by North Bridge. One had obviously been killed instantly, but the other appeared to have been scalped.

It was discovered later that just after the fight a boy with a hatchet in his hand had crossed the bridge from the Concord side to join the Americans. As he went by, a wounded British soldier was sitting up and trying to

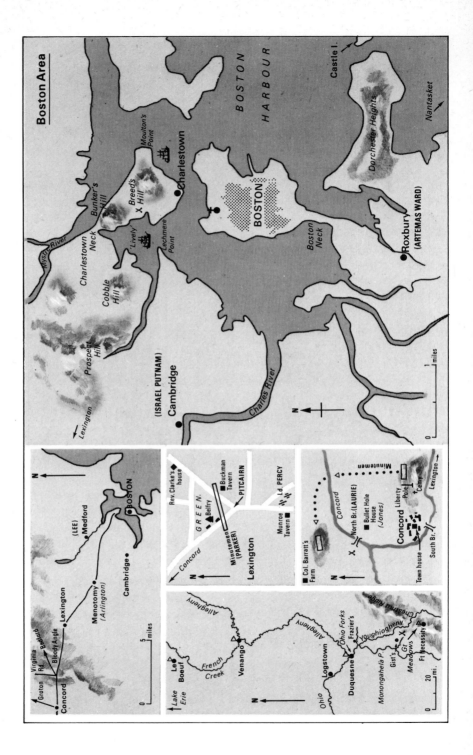

Boston Area

BOSTON HARBOUR

Castle I.

Nantasket

Dorchester Heights

BOSTON

Boston Neck

Roxbury
(ARTEMAS WARD)

Charlestown

Moulton's Point

Breed's Hill

Bunker's Hill

Charlestown Neck

'Lively'

Lechmere Point

Cobble Hill

Prospect Hill

Mystic River

Lexington

Cambridge
(ISRAEL PUTNAM)

Charles River

N

miles

N

BOSTON

Medford

(LEE)

Menotomy
(Arlington)

Cambridge

Lexington

Bloody Angle

Bedford

Virginia Rd.

Groton

Concord

5 miles

Lexington

Rev. Clarke's house

Buckman Tavern

PITCAIRN

G R E E N.

Belfry

Minuteman (PARKER)

Concord

Munroe Tavern

Ld. PERCY

N

Concord

Minutemen

Concord

North Br.(LAURIE)

Bullet Hole House (Jones)

Liberty Pole

Cem.

Lexington

Col. Barratt's Farm

X

South Br.

Town house

N

Lake Erie

Le Boeuf

French Creek

Venango

Allegheny

Allegheny

Ohio Forks

Frazier's

Logstown

Duquesne

Ohio

Monongahela R.

Youghiogheny

Gist's

Gt. Meadows

X

Ft. Necessity

Chestnut Ridge

N

20 mi.

raise himself to his knees. Then the boy, doubtless under the spell of the exciting action that had just taken place, and possibly fearing the soldier would attack him, finished off the unfortunate man by sinking the sharp blade of his weapon into his skull. This incident was to lead to exaggerated accounts of the Americans' barbarism. People in England were soon convinced that the rebels scalped their adversaries in Indian fashion.

*

Colonel Smith spent an hour or so consolidating and waiting for the hoped-for relief force from Boston to join up with him. Finally, he decided that time was working on the side of the rebels, and he turned his men about and led them back towards Lexington.

As soon as the troops had formed column of march and set off for home, the rebels, of whom there were now a great number in the vicinity, closed in. Crouching behind hedges, buildings and any cover they could find beside the roadway, they opened a brisk fire on the massed redcoats. Smith sent out flankers and from time to time the men in the column returned fire; but the rebels had the best of it. Safe behind cover they hardly suffered at all while many soldiers were killed or wounded and several officers were wounded. The worst moment was when passing the junction of the Virginia Road and the Old Bedford Road, some three miles east of Concord. Americans under the cover of forest growth opened up a devastating fire that killed eight soldiers outright, and wounded many more. Fittingly, this sharply curving section of the road where so much slaughter took place was known as the 'Bloody Angle'. But the losses were not all on one side. For example, in the heat of the action the British flankers were forgotten and Captain Wilson and two of his militiamen were killed by them, coming up unseen from the rear.

While approaching Lexington, the soldiers met Captain Parker's men again; but this time, the Americans were lining the hedgerows and had the advantage.

A quarter of a mile further down the road the redcoats reached the Bull Tavern, and a number forced an entry and seized the liquor in the bar.

Soon after this, the retreat having become almost a rout, Colonel Smith made an effort to rally his men. A strong rearguard was placed on a bluff to the north of the road while an attempt was made to form up the column again. Ensign de Bernière writes: 'When we arrived within a mile of Lexington our ammunition began to fail, and the light companies were so fatigued with flanking that they were scarce able to act, and the number of wounded scarce able to get forward made a great confusion. Colonel

Smith had received a wound through his leg, a number of officers were also wounded . . . and the men were beginning to run rather than retreat in order. We attempted to stop the men and form them two deep but at first to no purpose. At last, however, after we got through Lexington, the officers got to the front and presented their bayonets [sic] and told the men that if they advanced they should die. Upon this they began to form under heavy fire.'

*

General Percy with the relief force had by this time arrived at the eastern end of Lexington. Establishing his headquarters at the Munroe Tavern, he placed the 4th Regiment in position in line across the road to hold back the pursuers while Smith's column came through. After the men from Concord had all passed inside the line thrown out by their rescuers, the two field pieces with the relief party were brought into action on either side of the road, and men were sent forward to burn down and destroy the houses being used by rebel snipers. In this way the Americans were held off and Smith's column given a chance of reforming in an orderly fashion.

When the retreat was resumed the 23rd Regiment from the relief force formed the rearguard. Lieutenant Mackenzie of the 23rd recorded his impressions: 'As the country for miles round Boston and in the neighbourhood of Lexington and Concord had by this time had notice of what was doing, as well as by the firing, numbers of armed men on foot and on horseback were continually coming from all parts guided by the fire, and before the column had advanced a mile on the road, we were fired at from all quarters, particularly from the houses on the roadside and adjacent stone walls. Several of the troops were killed and wounded in this way, and the soldiers were so enraged at suffering from an unseen enemy that they forced open many of the houses from which the fire proceeded and put to death all those found in them. Those houses would certainly have been burnt had any fire been found in them, or had there been time to kindle any; but only three or four near where we first formed suffered in this way . . . Our regiment having formed the rearguard for near seven miles, and expended a great deal of its ammunition, was then relieved by the Marines which was the next battalion in the column.'

Lord Percy had planned to return via Cambridge and Roxbury; but fearing the important bridge over the Charles River at Cambridge might have been tampered with[1], he changed his mind and made for Charles-

---

[1] Lord Percy's judgement was correct. The planks had been taken up and the far end was defended by minutemen.

The retreat of the British from Concord by Alonzo Chappel

town and the water-crossing to Boston. During the whole of the march from Lexington, the rebels kept up an incessant fire on the column, and on several occasions closed in crying out, 'King Hancock for ever;' but few women and children were seen throughout the day, and the rebels had probably removed most of their families from the neighbourhood. As soon as the troops had passed Charlestown Neck the rebels ceased firing, the houses close to the Neck being their last position. The return of the shattered column down the peninsula and over the water to Boston was unmolested.

Chapter Three

THE SIEGE OF BOSTON

'Search the vast volumes of history through, and I much question whether a case similar to ours is to be found; to wit, to maintain a post against the flower of the British troops for six months together, without powder, and at the end of them to have one army disbanded and another to raise within the same distance of a reinforced enemy.'

George Washington in a letter written to the President of the Continental Congress in January 1776.

The encounters on the Concord road were followed by a full-scale operation against Breed's Hill on the Charlestown Peninsula which the rebels had been bold enough to occupy. It had been the idea of Israel Putnam, or 'Old Put' as he was called, to man the hill. With the blessing of the local Committee of Safety but the by no means enthusiastic consent of the rebels' commander Artemas Ward, he had been allowed to assemble some of his Connecticut men and a larger body from Massachusetts for the purpose. Yet when the time came to march, 'Old Put' was not placed in charge. The Massachusetts men liked him personally, but after all he came from Connecticut, so they persuaded the Committee of Safety to appoint William Prescott, in whom everyone had confidence.

That evening they arrived at Charlestown Neck, and Prescott and Putnam went into conference as to what they were going to do. The problem was that their orders told them to take possession of Bunker's Hill; but Breed's Hill, which was sometimes referred to as part of Bunker's Hill, was nearer to Boston and in a more commanding position.

After some hesitation a decision was arrived at. Prescott and the main body skirted Bunker's Hill and climbed to the top of Breed's Hill, while Putnam led a detachment forward and occupied Bunker's Hill. Thereafter, Putnam's men achieved almost nothing as regards entrenching their position[1]; but those on Breed's Hill set about it with a will and by dawn a

[1] It seems that Putnam asked Prescott to send him back some entrenching tools. Prescott agreed to do so provided the men sent with them returned. In the event Putnam got the tools and did not use them and the men skulked off back to camp.

General Israel Putnam by John Trumbull

formidable redoubt had been built which, had powerful cannon been able to be emplaced, would have dominated Boston.

There were British warships at anchor in the waters around the Charlestown Peninsula, and a look-out aboard the *Lively* was the first to see the fully fledged fort on the top of the hill where the night before there had been no fort at all. The captain was called, and then Admiral Graves was signalled, after which, an order having been given to open fire on the fort, General Gage was informed.

About this time Generals Howe, Clinton and Burgoyne had arrived and Gage asked the senior of his new assistants to reconnoitre the position and submit a plan to evict the enemy.

In a reconnaissance from midstream, Howe noticed that although the redoubt was very strong, some low walls and a fence leading down to the shore of the Mystic River, which were also manned, offered the possibility of a break-through. He thus considered a feint at the redoubt coupled with a thrust towards the fence would be the best way to drive the rebels from Breed's Hill. At the council of war which followed, Clinton, pointing to a map, suggested it would be easier to pinch off the whole peninsula by seizing Charlestown Neck. Gage did not approve of Clinton's idea as it would put the British force between two bodies of the enemy. He liked Howe's plan, however, and ordered him to carry it out.

Howe's force began crossing at half-past one on 17 June 1775; in twenty-eight barges manned by the navy; in two parallel columns of fourteen each. They landed by Moulton's Point below Moulton Hill, an excellent landing site with a wide shallow beach. The redcoats, forty odd to each barge, scrambled out and formed up while the craft returned for more, still keeping in perfect order. The second batch contained, besides more redcoats, some blue-jacketed artillerymen with their six-pounders; it also included General Howe and his staff.

After Howe had stepped ashore he looked towards the vulnerable enemy wing he intended to attack. Moving down the hill towards the fence was a body of men. Howe concluded the rebels were strengthening their position by the shore; but he nevertheless decided to continue with his plan.

*

Howe advanced his men slowly against the enemy position. He considered a stolid, grim advance would intimidate the rebels. Had there been any artillery opposition he would not have dared to do this, but the rebels only managed to loose a few balls from the pair of four-pounders in the redoubt, and these sailed over the heads of the soldiers to plop harmlessly in Boston Bay. Howe's own artillery was almost as ineffective, for twelve-pounder balls had been brought by mistake, and only grape could be used until replacements had been secured. While the British centre and left climbed slowly up the hill towards the redoubt, the more important right moved purposefully along the shore towards the fence, which though now stuffed with hay, still offered poor protection to the rebels.

With the latter, the hardest task was to prevent the inexperienced militia from firing too soon. Those manning the flimsy defences stretching towards the Mystic were told not to fire until the redcoats reached a stick placed in the ground thirty-five yards ahead of them; while to the men in the redoubt—according to one tradition—Prescott gave the famous order, 'Don't shoot until you see the whites of their eyes.'[1] The result by the shore was most impressive. When the 23rd and 4th Regiments

[1] This has also been attributed to Putnam. It seems unlikely. He was presumably back on Bunker's Hill.

passed the stick they were met with such a blast that it was as if they had collided with a cliff. They reeled back in disorder, licking their wounds. Their comrades in the feint attack on the left then retired in sympathy; and the result was that in a matter of minutes the whole British force was back by the landing place.

All thought of outflanking the Americans was now given up. Instead, a frontal assault on the redoubt was ordered. The first men to attack were stopped in their tracks by a blast from Prescott's men at point-blank range as formidable as that which had met their comrades by the shore. But Howe was not willing to let a bunch of peasants stop his regulars. He brought up reserves, consolidated his shaken lines, and ordered the redoubt to be stormed regardless of the cost.

This final time, the redcoats again met a blast of musketry that caused them to waver; but powder was running out, and the following volley was only a splutter. Pressing on, some of the redcoats climbed into the redoubt; and the rebels, grasping their muskets, then slipped through the open back of the defence-work and away. Prescott was one of the last to leave, walking backwards slowly, parrying with his sword the bayonets thrust towards him. Dr. Warren, although nominally a general, had volunteered to take his place in the line. He too withdrew from the redoubt; but did not manage to get far. His body, a bullet through the head, was found later behind the breastwork. Meanwhile, the heroes by the shore were getting away almost unmolested.

Having driven the rebels from the hill, the British occupied Charlestown which had been burnt out during the battle. They then spread over the whole peninsula. But they did not follow the rebels to the mainland. Shocked by their heavy casualties, which were more than twice those of the Americans, they were not anxious to attempt anything more for the moment.

*

It was while Washington was in New York, on his way to Boston, that he received the news of the battle. Cheered by the accounts of the gallantry of the colonials, he immediately hurried forward to New England to assume command. On the afternoon of his arrival he rode out to Prospect Hill in the north of the American position to view the area. On Bunker's Hill two miles to the east were British sentinels, the first redcoats he had seen since his Ohio days, and below were the blackened ruins of Charlestown, also manned; to the north-east in the estuary of the Mystic floating batteries lay at anchor; while in the opposite direction was Boston itself,

Artemas Ward, engraving after
Charles Willson Peale

looking like the footprint of some monster on its queer-shaped peninsula; finally, in the harbour beyond, lay the British fleet riding easily on the summer tide. After a quick glance at the enemy side, Washington took a look at his own, and noticed that the American redoubts were mostly ill-constructed and often badly placed. However, some of the positions were naturally strong, and he concluded that 'with vigor and good engineering' he might be able to create a line at least strong enough to confine the British within Boston while he set about the task of training his troops.

*

A few days later Washington made a fuller inspection of the American lines, this time in the company of his subordinate commanders. These were Charles Lee in command of the sector opposite the Charlestown Peninsula, Israel Putnam leading the centre, and his predecessor Artemas Ward who was now in charge of the right wing opposite Boston Neck.

Washington began by visiting the camps, and was appalled at the ramshackle huts, sloppy sentries and general air of mess and disorder. He next

Frontier rifleman

inspected some of the Connecticut and Massachusetts regiments in the vicinity of Roxbury. The discipline of none of these was good by professional standards, but was least bad, as always, where the officers were intelligent and alert. Arms were poor and of every age and type, powder was woefully short, and many of the men who had lost clothing at Bunker's Hill had not had it replaced as promised. It was manifest, too, that many officers did not know their duties. Washington had already sensed this, and before riding out to inspect the lines had explained to Congress in a letter, that although it was too much to expect troops just assembled from civilian life 'to possess the order, regularity and discipline of veterans', yet he hoped that deficiencies would 'soon be made up by the activity and zeal of the officers and the docility and obedience of the men'.

Washington began his task of sharpening up discipline by trying to improve the quality of the officers on whom he believed everything depended. A fault he found, and attempted to eradicate, was the practice of 'levelling'; that is treating the officers and men as equals. A gent-

Daniel Morgan

leman himself, he thought officers should be gentlemen, or at least behave like them. Only in this way, he believed, could proper discipline be maintained. Another habit he disliked was having the men elect their leaders, a practice prevalent in Massachusetts. He considered it led to the currying of favour from those entitled to do the choosing.

*

Washington's task of improving discipline was made more difficult by the arrival in camp of some of the frontier riflemen Congress had recruited on the recommendation of General Charles Lee. Lee had spoken of their potentialities as soldiers in glowing terms, extolling 'their amazing hardihood, their methods of living so long in the woods without carrying provisions with them, the exceeding quickness with which they can march to distant parts, and, above all, the dexterity to which they had arrived in the use of the rifle gun'. Lee added, almost with awe: 'There is not one of these men who wish a distance less than 200 yards or a larger object than an orange. Every shot is fatal.'[1] They certainly arrived re-

---

[1] I. Ballagh, Lee's Letters 130–131.

Soldier in a hunting shirt

markably quickly. Stephenson's men from the vicinity of Berkeley County, Virginia marched thirty to thirty-six miles a day and even then never caught up with Daniel Morgan's party whom they were supposed to accompany. They shot well too. On arrival, a nose outlined in chalk on a board was obliterated by the first forty making the test. By the time the whole company had shot, the board itself was blown in bits from the tree. The men were fine physical specimens, and all were clad in the service-able hunters' shirts which Washington had persuaded General Forbes to adopt as far back as 1758. What they lacked, however, was discipline. They saw one duty and one only. That was to kill the British precisely as their fathers had slain the Indians. As soon as these 'shirtmen' as the others called them were established in their camps, they began to slip off through the line of guards and make their way towards the British outposts. Some went alone; a few crept forward in pairs. Whenever they spotted a red-coat they would take aim even if he was at the furthest range of their rifles. The result was much wastage of powder and no increase in British casualties. This endless pop-pop by the riflemen at extreme distance was the main reason for Washington's stern order of 4 August 1775 against futile firing.

*

By September, Washington was not far from the point where he could say that his army was improving. He began to feel he might be able soon to do more with his 19,000 men than just drill them and keep them waiting behind parapets; and several plans for aggressive action formed in his mind. First, now that he had stopped all deliveries into Boston from the countryside, he considered arming some schooners and trying to cut off supplies coming by sea. Second, he decided to give any help required to General Schuyler if that quasi-independent commander in Albany was able to carry out the decision Congress had reached before Washington left Philadelphia and to invade Canada. Third, he wanted if possible to deliver a direct attack of his own on Boston.

The action at sea where the British were so strong was surprisingly successful. In the second week of October Washington received reports from Philadelphia that 'two north country built brigs of no force', one of which was named the *Nancy*, had left England bound for Quebec laden with arms, and other stores. The American schooner *Lee* had already left to prey on British shipping, and had managed to recapture a vessel laden with timber that a British prize crew was taking to Boston. Having been alerted about the brigs, the *Lee* went in search of them. By the luckiest of chances she made contact with the *Nancy* well out at sea. She boarded her; but in sight of her consort who, putting on all sail, made off for Boston. As the British would soon learn of the *Nancy's* fate, and probably try and recapture her, she was taken to a nearby Massachusetts port. She proved a prize indeed. Although she carried no powder, there were 2,000 stand of small arms aboard, many flints, several tons of musket shot, and a trophy of special esteem and utility, a fine large brass mortar. When before long this long giant was brought to Cambridge, General Putnam christened it with a bottle of rum and named it 'The Congress'.

The Canadian venture also started satisfactorily, for Schuyler's force under General Montgomery quickly advanced north past Lake Champlain and captured Montreal. Washington's column however did not do so well. It was commanded by the fiery Benedict Arnold, who had earlier won renown by capturing Ticonderoga in partnership with Ethan Allen and his Green Mountain Boys. Arnold advanced on Quebec by a difficult easterly route along the Kennebec and Claudière rivers. He reached the fort with part of his force and managed to join up with the column from Montreal; but, in the joint attack, General Montgomery was killed, and the Americans were repulsed with heavy losses.

*

On 8 September 1775, Washington called a council of war to decide whether an assault should be made on Boston. Lee was not able to attend but wrote saying he thought it should. However, his fellow commanders disagreed. They considered that the British positions on Boston Neck were too strong, and the Neck too narrow for there to be any chance of success in a land attack; while if an attempt were made by boat across the Bay it would be 'sheer murder'. In any case, they stated, an early change of government in England with the possible repeal of the Boston Port Act seemed likely; and as this would make an attack unnecessary, it would be best to await the arrival of the next ship which might very well bring the announcement of the King's dismissal of Lord North.[1] The minutes recorded that the council was unanimous. Unanimous was not quite correct, for Lee had approved of an attack, as did Washington at heart. 'I cannot say,' the latter reported to Congress afterwards, 'that I have wholly laid aside the idea.'

*

In October came word that General Gage had been ordered home and General Howe appointed head of the armed forces in New England. As far as Washington was concerned there was no ground for rejoicing over the transfer of command. After all, Howe had shown an aggressive spirit at Breed's Hill and might very well prove more formidable than Gage had been. This fact Washington had to bear in mind as he considered an appeal just received from Congress asking him to attack Boston 'as soon as a favourable opportunity opens'.

   Although a council of war had recently decided that the army should not attempt to storm Boston, Washington felt he would now have to submit the question to his senior officers. He consequently called them together and told them he had 'an intimation from the Congress that an attack on Boston, if practicable, was much to be desired'. Again, the generals did not believe it feasible. Nathanael Greene, one of Washington's favourites, thought it could only be successful if 10,000 men were landed in Boston. John Sullivan considered the winter a more suitable time. Even Charles Lee now thought it too great a risk; and the others said simply that it was impracticable. Washington, therefore, gave up the idea.

---

[1] The gist of 18 Papers of G.W. 30 LC, printed in 3 Force (4) p. 768.

Instead, he turned the whole of his attention to a grave crisis in manpower that was developing.

*

The problem was that under the terms of their enlistment the Connecticut regiments with a total strength of 3,700 would be due to return to civilian life on the first day of December; and early reports indicated that very few of the rank and file would re-enlist, or even agree to stay on until the end of the month when the Massachusetts and New Hampshire troops were also due to leave. Washington, therefore, had not only to create a new army by the first day of January 1776; but also to try and replace the Connecticut men or induce them to stay on a little while longer. Every effort was made to persuade the Connecticut men to forgo their rights for the sake of the cause. All in vain. They insisted on leaving, and were strengthened in their resolve when cold weather came and they compared their miserable huts with the warm homes awaiting them. The Continental Congress had suggested that militia should be enrolled to fill the gap caused by the Connecticut men's departure. Washington was very loth to adopt this solution. He remembered only too well how unreliable the militia had been in his days on the Virginian frontier. In the end, however, he sent out the calls to Massachusetts and New Hampshire to enrol militia to come to his aid. And the response was rewarding. Connecticut's defection encouraged the other two colonies to show what they could do. In record time 5,000 of their 'Long Faces'—as militia were derisively termed—arrived at Cambridge. They received the warmest of welcomes; and this was in contrast to the resentment shown the departing Connecticut contingents. As Charles Lee wrote: 'The Connecticut men marched off bag and baggage, but in passing through the lines of other regiments they were so horridly hissed, groaned at and pelted that I believe they wished their aunts, grandmothers and even sweethearts to whom the day before they were so much attached at the Devil's own place.'

On 4 January the force Washington had under arms was said to be 10,000; less than half the authorized strength, in spite of all his efforts at recruitment. Nevertheless he set about creating a sound organisation for those he had; and to help morale hoisted a union flag with thirteen red and white strips in honour of the united colonies. Soon after the flag was raised aloft, there was received the long-awaited text of the King's speech from the throne to both Houses of Parliament in October 1775. This showed there was no change of policy. The monarch announced his intention of putting a speedy end to the rebellious war. For this purpose he had increased his army and navy and received the most friendly offers of foreign assistance—by which no doubt he meant he had hired troops from German states. He promised pardons to any colony disposed to return to its allegiance, and gave a hint of free trade, protection and security as if it had never revolted.[1]

In spite of the concessions, the King's speech met with nothing but ridicule from Washington and his army. The Tories in Boston, however, noticing the Union Jack in the mast quarter of the flag with the stripes, wrongly assumed their rebel comrades had read the King's Speech and raised it as a symbol of submission.

Meanwhile, Lee had gone off to Rhode Island to try to persuade some leading Tories to change their standpoint and take an oath of allegiance to the Continental Congress. On his return he brought the news that the British in Boston were fitting out a fleet to go to New York and expressed the opinion that the city should be occupied.

Washington had considered the possibility of the British descending on New York. He had asked Congress whether in such an event he should detach troops, should await instructions, or should rely on the men of the nearby colonies to defend the city.[2] No answer had been given and, now that a British move there seemed in the making, Washington dispatched an urgent message to Congress suggesting a watchful eye should be kept on the city and New Jersey troops be sent in. More than this he did not think he should do because of his lack of familiarity with conditions in New York.

Distance and circumstance had made Washington's position as commander-in-chief more nominal than directional. Besides which he was not sure he should exercise all the powers his title seemed to confer. Learning of this, Lee put forward his own views on the matter. 'I have the greatest reason to believe,' he said, 'and from the most authentic intelligence, that the best members of Congress expect that you would take much upon yourself; as referring everything to them is, in fact, defeating the project.'[3] And then, he immediately made to Washington a detailed proposal for the occupation of New York and the nearby countryside.

Lee's plan appealed to the commander-in-chief; but he still remained in doubt as to his authority. As John Adams happened to be at hand

[1] Dodsley's Annual Register, 1775, p. 269 ff.

[2] 4. G.W. 24–25.

[3] 1 Lee Papers, 234.

Washington decided to consult him. Adam's reply was immediate and unequivocal: Washington should seize New York; it was entirely within his authority to do so; he was vested with full power and authority to act as he should think fit for the good and welfare of the service.[1] This satisfied Washington, and he at once gave Lee instructions to proceed to New York and put it 'into the best position of defence which the season and circumstances will permit of'.[2]

*

The day after he gave Lee his orders, Washington received the first detailed returns of his new army. He had estimated from incomplete weekly figures that the total would be 10,500, or about forty-five per cent of the number authorized, but was appalled to learn that enlistments were only 8,212, and the number of men actually present and fit for duty a mere 5,582.

Washington had by now firmly decided to make an attack on Boston, and was determined to acquire sufficient forces to do so with success. He, therefore, immediately called a council of war to decide how the additional troops might be raised, and, in addition, the form the attack should take. He asked John Adams and the other representatives from Congress present to attend, along with his general officers; and on 16 January 1776 laid before them 'a state of the regiments of the Continental Army, the consequent weakness of his lines, and in his judgment, the indispensable necessity of making a bold attempt to conquer the ministerial troops in Boston before they can be reinforced in the spring, if the means can be provided, and a favourable opportunity offered'.[3] In fact, he asked the council for their views.

Whether it was due to Washington's determined mien, or the presence of the delegates from Congress, is not clear; but this time there were no doubters. It was speedily agreed that an attack should be made as soon as practicable; and to facilitate it Washington was authorized to call for thirteen militia regiments to serve from 1 February to the end of March: seven from Massachusetts, four from Connecticut, and two from New Hampshire. The call went out accordingly; the response was good; and although a desperate shortage of arms and powder delayed the attack, the opportune arrival of Henry Knox with fifty-two cannon, nine large mortars and five cohorns, skilfully hauled over the snow from Fort Ticonde-

[1] Letter of 6 Jan 1776; 1 LTW.
[2] 4. G.W. 218.
[3] 4 Force (4) 774–5.

roga, soon allowed Washington to set about preparing for his operation against Boston.

*

On 13 February Washington went to Lechmere Point near Charlestown Neck and looked over towards Boston. He found the water frozen solid all the way across the channel—so heavily frozen in fact that some soldiers at the fort on the point were making it a business to go out on the ice and pick up the spent balls the British troops had fired in their direction, one American boasting he had recovered eighty. Seeing this as a new way to reach Boston, Washington conceived the idea that an attack might be made over the ice; but when he put the plan to his generals, they were all against it.

Washington next suggested the occupation either of Noodle's Island in the north of the Bay or of the Dorchester Heights peninsula in the south, with the object of luring the enemy into making a sortie. There was general approval for this idea, and after a discussion the Dorchester area was selected because of its nearby land approach.

The final plan of attack evolved by the Americans was a complicated one. There was to be an initial bombardment of Boston from the batteries at Cobble Hill and Lechmere Point in the north and Lamb's Dam in the south; and this was to be followed by the occupation and entrenchment of the Dorchester Heights. Finally, a substantial force was to be assembled in the vicinity of Cambridge with the task of crossing in boats and attacking Boston if the British came out and started to assault the positions established on the Dorchester Heights.

In the event things went almost exactly as the Americans had hoped. The bombardment indeed was not very effective; but on the other hand the reply proved even less so, for a number of the British shells burst in flight and many others did not explode at all.[1] The Dorchester Heights were occupied under cover of darkness without interference, and providentially the ground was found to have thawed out sufficiently for trenches to be dug. Then in the morning, when the British first became conscious of the new American redoubts on the hills so close to them, they found they could not elevate their cannon sufficiently to blast the intruders out, and most of their projectiles fell harmlessly below the crest.

The occupation of the Dorchester Heights tempted the British to come out and attack, for after a council of war General Howe decided to try and storm the Americans out of their new strongholds. He ordered one

[1] Barker's Diary.

force to go by water on the night tide to Castle Island to assault the eastern tip of the Dorchester Heights, and he instructed another body of men to cross by flat-boats and attack the north face. The British might very well have succeeded in their designs. But providentially for the Americans before they could do so a fierce storm arose. At nightfall it became obvious that vessels would not be able to disembark troops on Castle Island because of the high seas; and also that any flat-bottomed boats heading for the north face would be swamped. Reluctantly, therefore, when there were no signs of the storm abating, Howe called off the attack.

*

During the days following the storm Washington noticed that the British were making preparations for some move, but could not deduce what they were going to do. Then, on 8 March 1776, a delegation of the citizens of Boston under a flag of truce came out past the forward British post on Boston Neck and delivered a message saying that General Howe had decided to leave Boston and would not destroy the city unless his troops were molested during their departure.[1] Because the message did not bear Howe's signature, and there was doubt as to its authenticity, Washington did not send back a formal acceptance of the terms offered; but as it seemed likely the British were in fact about to leave, he ordered a start to be made on further entrenchments in a more forward position on the Heights so that if Howe changed his mind, or lingered unduly, he might be blasted more easily out of the port.

*

Nothing much happened until Sunday, 10 March 1776. Then soldiers were seen loading vessels at the wharves, and one ship after another began raising sail and making for Castle Island and the Nantasket Roads. The following day more ships left; and in face of adverse winds relied on the tide to wash them down channel to Nantasket. Nevertheless, the grip of the redcoats on the town appeared to remain unbroken. 'The arrogant roll of distant drum, the change of guard, the flapping of the King's flag on Beacon Hill—all these marked the daily round of occupation.'[2] On 15 March the impatient Americans had to endure the news that the wind was favourable but the British still loitered; and on the 16th to accept that the wind had shifted so adversely they could not leave at all. But on 17 March, with the wind favourable again, the wharves became thronged.

[1] 4 G.W. 377n.

[2] 4 Freeman 49.

Troops were first seen entering their boats, and then making for vessels riding at anchor close by. These ships later spread their canvas and sailed down to join the rest at Nantasket. On the night of 19–20 March the British were heard demolishing the defences on Castle Island, blowing up the buildings that could not be burned.

British troops

Several uneventful days dragged by. The 27th dawned with a promise of spring in the air and a fair wind from the north-west. At eleven o'clock in the morning the flagship *Fowey* hoisted signal. Then, at three o'clock, the whole fleet weighed anchor, made sail from Nantasket, and put out to sea.

*

The British ships, along with 1,000 Boston Tories aboard, were making for Halifax, Nova Scotia. Washington, however, was convinced they were going towards the Hudson. So convinced that he sent his Continentals marching in that direction. In the event he proved to be wise, for it was not long before the British sailed down to assault New York.

Chapter Four

NEW YORK

Washington found it extremely difficult to decide on the best course to take. The advice of General Greene was to burn the town. 'Two-thirds belong to the Tories,' he said, 'so we have no great reason to run any risk for its defence, and burning it will deprive the enemy of an opportunity of barracking the whole army together.' Congress, however, would not allow the destruction of New York and told Washington it must be held 'at every hazard'.

[1]

Before the battle of New York, General Cornwallis joined the British forces in America. He was the son of the first Earl Cornwallis of Brome Hall in Suffolk, and after leaving Eton received a commission in the Grenadier Guards. Following a short spell at a military academy at Turin, he saw service in Germany under the Marquess of Granby in the Seven Years War; and in 1761 at the age of twenty-three was given command of the 12th Regiment of Foot[1]. On succeeding his father in 1769 he left the army to manage the family estates. Entering Parliament he supported the Rockingham ministry and in recognition for his services was made a privy councillor in 1770 and Constable of the Tower of London in 1771. Cornwallis was one of a tiny minority of five peers who, during the recurring crises in America, showed sympathy towards the colonials, but this did not prevent him going out to help repress the rebellion.

*

With the rank of lieutenant general, Cornwallis left for America in February 1776 in a convoy crammed with troops bound for Wilmington on the Cape Fear River in North Carolina. The object of the expedition was to join up with General Clinton who had left Boston with a similar fleet and give support to the Southern Loyalists. Dispersed by a storm, the ships from England did not meet up with those from Boston until early in

[1] Later the Suffolk Regiment.

Lord Cornwallis by Thomas Gainsborough

May 1776, by which time the American commander[1] in the area had trounced the Tories, and scattered them to the back country. When the British eventually joined up off the coast of the Carolinas any immediate opportunity of helping the Loyalists was gone. But Clinton was loth to leave without doing something; and believing Charleston might provide a base for future operations he attempted to capture the port.

*

Access to the inner harbour at Charleston was made extremely hazardous by the guns of Fort Moultrie on the tip of Sullivan Island, east of the passage of entry, and after appreciating the situation, Clinton decided to land his invasion force on Long Island which lay east of Sullivan Island, and then move across and try and take Fort Moultrie in the rear. Long Island and Sullivan Island were separated by a narrow channel which was reported to have a depth of eighteen inches. After the landing had been successfully made, however, it was discovered to be seven feet deep. There were no boats to take the army across and no way of reaching the objec-

[1] Charles Lee.

tive presented itself, so, in a change of plan, Clinton asked the naval commander to move in the warships and bombard the fort into submission. For once, however, the British were outgunned and the ships suffered more than the fort. By this time the British were thoroughly disheartened so, as soon as the troops had reboarded the transports, and there was a favourable wind, the fleet made for New York.

*

Admiral Lord Howe and his brother General Sir William Howe had already sailed down from Halifax, Nova Scotia and encamped a British force on Staten Island a few miles from New York. By the middle of August, after more men had arrived from Europe, there were as many as 32,000 troops on the island. These included 8,000 from Germany, who although drawn from Brunswick, Hanover, Hesse-Hanau, Hesse-Cassel and Wandeck, were all called indiscriminately Hessians. According to Sir George Collier in the *Rainbow* which accompanied them the Germans had an unpleasant crossing to America. First, because of thick weather, the transports became separated. Then, fogs off Newfoundland made it even more difficult to keep together, and the result was that when the weather cleared off Nova Scotia seventeen sail were missing.

After the British troops had left Boston and made for Halifax it was expected they would remain in Canada until reinforced from England, so the convoy carrying the Germans headed in that direction. It was not until they were approaching the harbour that they heard to their chagrin that Howe and his army had already left for New York. Sir George Collier writes: 'This was disagreeable news for the sick men of whom there were already great numbers, and who, after a tedious and uncomfortable voyage of nine weeks, were in hopes of meeting with a little quiet and refreshment. The expectation, however, was illusive; for as the service would not admit of any delay, the fleet, without anchoring, turned their prows to the southward and shaped for New York. This passage again was very tedious, for calms, contrary winds and currents drove the fleet in such adverse directions as baffling every reckoning. The commander of the Germans, old General von Heister, who was embarked on board a merchant ship, exhausted his whole stock of tobacco and patience together. He wrote a letter couched in terms of grief, impatience and despair. "I have been imposed on and deceived," said the old veteran; "for I was assured the voyage would not exceed six or seven weeks. It is now more than fourteen since I embarked, and full three months since I left England, yet I see no more prospect of landing than I did after our sailing. I am an old man, covered with wounds, and imbecilitated by age and fatigues, and it is impossible I should survive if the voyage continued much longer."'

Sir George goes on to say that he then went on board the transport to visit and comfort the old general; and to do it more effectively than by words, he carried him 'refreshments and provisions, but above all plenty of tobacco', the absence of which he learned was the principal cause of the veteran's dejection. This and an assurance that the voyage would soon be over seem to have raised the old man's spirits considerably. He ordered the band to play, called for hock, and swallowed large potations, drinking the health of the King of England, the Landgrave and his many other friends.

After a passage of many weeks from England the convoy eventually arrived at the mouth of the Hudson and the Germans were able to disembark and go into camp alongside their British allies; and on a happier note, Sir George concludes: 'The plenty of refreshment they received soon recovered them from the fatigues of their long voyage and rendered them perfectly fit for service.'

*

New York had been selected as the principal objective of the coming British offensive because it had a strong loyalist sentiment, was centrally located on the Atlantic coast, possessed a fine harbour, and formed a good base for an advance up the Hudson which, combined with a thrust down from Canada past Lake Champlain, might very well split the colonies into two parts.

The Howes had been empowered to act as peace commissioners as well as battle commanders and thus made an initial attempt to come to terms with the rebels. But their efforts were hampered by an over-exact approach. They were not willing to recognise George Washington as a general in command of troops and addressed him as Mr. Washington. Washington for his part was not willing to enter into negotiations until his status was accepted. Admiral Howe managed eventually to obtain a meeting with Benjamin Franklin, John Adams and Edward Rutledge at his brother's headquarters on Staten Island. But by the time this was arranged there had been developments which made conciliation almost impossible; the colonists were in the process of announcing their independence. On 2 July 1776 a committee of the Continental Congress sitting in Philadelphia placed before the full assembly a document composed by Thomas Jefferson of Pennsylvania and John Adams of Massachusetts

which both summarised the injustices suffered by the thirteen colonies at the hands of George III and set out succinctly the reasons why the colonies had a basic right to be free and independent.

The committee's draft was well received by the full assembly and the views it expressed were speedily endorsed. So quickly was this carried out, in fact, that only two days later, on 4 July, Congress was able to declare the country's independence to the American people and the world.

*

After it had become clear that a peaceful settlement was not possible the Howes began planning their attack on New York. On 12 July the Admiral made a probe at the defences of the city by sending two frigates up the Hudson River. The American defenders made little attempt to prevent the vessels' passage. They stood idly by watching until the broadsides were fired. Then they scampered away from the shore batteries to seek safety in the town. For about a month the British ships remained anchored in the Tappan Zee to the north of the city, where they seriously disrupted communications with the American army in the Hudson Heights. On 3 August an attack in small boats was beaten off. On 16 August a fire-raft attack was also repulsed. But this came so close to success that shortly afterwards the little squadron withdrew to rejoin the main fleet off Staten Island.

After the naval reconnaissance had been completed the set-piece combined attack on Long Island was begun. As the sun rose on the morning of 22 August Admiral Howe's fleet stood in towards Long Island, menacing the shore with its cannon. In the waters off Staten Island scores of flatboats, bateaux and row-galleys next began to move. Under the guns of the fleet they crossed the Narrows and landed 4,000 redcoats in Gravesend Bay. The boats then went back for more and by noon had put 15,000 men ashore. Directly the vanguard had landed Cornwallis led it forward and seized the township of Flatbush. Some Pennsylvanian riflemen bivouacked near the point lay hidden in the cornfields during the landing, and they watched its progress anxiously. Then, after a short exchange of fire, they fell back to warn their comrades, burning crops and slaughtering cattle as they went in an effort to impede the British advance.

*

On the American side, hastily conceived plans had been made to receive the invaders. General Putnam was assigned the task of defending Long Island, and 'Old Put', having made his headquarters in the fortified lines of Brooklyn in the north, placed Sullivan with 3,500 men in position

The Declaration of Independence by John Trumbull

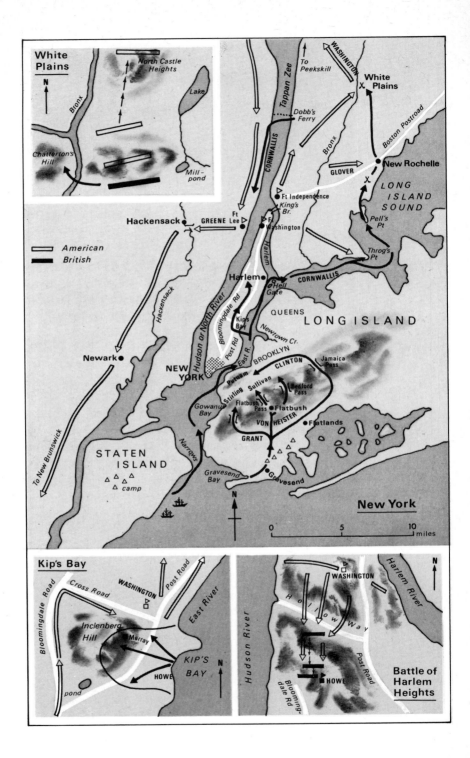

White Plains

North Castle Heights

Lake

Chatterton's Hill

Mill-pond

American
British

To Peekskill

WASHINGTON

White Plains

Tappan Zee

Dobb's Ferry

Bronx

Boston Postroad

New Rochelle

GLOVER

LONG ISLAND SOUND

Pell's Pt

CORNWALLIS

Ft Independence

King's Br.

Hackensack

GREENE

Ft Lee

Ft Washington

Harlem

Throg's Pt

Hackensack

Harlem

Hell Gate

CORNWALLIS

Bloomingdale Rd

QUEENS

LONG ISLAND

Kip's Bay

Newtown Cr.

Newark

Hudson or North River

Post Rd

East R.

BROOKLYN

CLINTON

Jamaica Pass

NEW YORK

Putnam

Stirling

Sullivan

Bedford Pass

Flatbush Pass

Flatbush

Gowanus Bay

VON HEISTER

Flatlands

GRANT

STATEN ISLAND

Narrows

Gravesend Bay

Gravesend

N

New York

△ camp

To New Brunswick

0   5   10 miles

Kip's Bay

Bloomingdale Road

Cross Road

WASHINGTON

Post Road

East River

Inclenberg Hill

Murray

HOWE

KIP'S BAY

N

pond

WASHINGTON

Harlem River

Hollow Way

Hudson River

Post Road

Bloomingdale Rd

HOWE

N

Battle of Harlem Heights

along the Long Island Heights, hoping that the ridge and its defenders would prove a serious obstacle for the invaders. Washington left the pre-battle preparations to his subordinates. He toured the forward line early on and then, seemingly satisfied, retired to Brooklyn.

The heights which run from east to west across the island were pene-trated in the centre by the Flatbush and Bedford passes and in the east by the Jamaica pass. Sullivan assumed personal command of the centre and its passes, and placed Lord Stirling in charge of the west flank and Colonel Miles on the east flank. He gave Miles no special instructions about defending the Jamaica pass, but a five-officer patrol was sent there to watch and warn.

*

On 26 August, four days after the landing, the British order of battle was changed. First, Von Heister took over the central sector north of Flatbush from Cornwallis and Grant moved across to the west to command the sector by the shore. Then, next day, very early and on an unseasonably chilly morning, the British offensive began. Von Heister's Hessians moved forward in a feint attack against the American outposts guarding the Flatbush and Bedford passes; Grant's division advanced along the coast road and struck at Stirling's men; and 10,000 men commanded per-sonally by Clinton and with Cornwallis's division in the lead set off east-wards to turn the American position.

By 3 a.m. the envelopers were approaching the Jamaica pass; and they caught the officer patrol there completely by surprise and secured the pass without firing a shot. Too late, Miles marched up with 500 of his men. He found an overwhelming British force installed and was quickly subdued. Clinton let his men have a short rest which enabled them to eat the cold breakfast brought in their knapsacks. After this the trail was cleared of trees to make it wide enough for wagons to go through the pass. At 7 a.m. the march was resumed, and when the column was safely through, Clinton ordered two cannon shots to be fired to tell Von Heister in the centre and Grant by the shore that the flank march had been successfully completed.

*

When the Americans facing the Hessians in the centre realised they were almost surrounded they began to lose heart. The sight of German bay-onets in front combined with the knowledge that redcoats were behind demoralised them. Slowly at first, men started to trickle away to safety. Then streams of them began to run for the wooded hills in the rear of

Stirling's brigades by the shore. As one man after another 'pulled foot', his neighbours caught the disease. Soon a flood of terrified soldiers were racing towards the earthworks and bastions of Brooklyn.

Sullivan, finally realising all was lost, gave an official order to the remainder of his men to fall back. But their departure proved no more orderly than that of their predecessors. As they went, men threw away their muskets, their packs, their blankets. Some ran off along any path they could find; others hid themselves in thickets. Eventually, only Sullivan, his staff and some few hundred of the stauncher ones were left, and before long these were surrounded and captured.

The crumbling of the American centre and the disintegration of the eastern flank left Stirling and his men facing the entire British invasion force alone. They put up a better resistance than the others had done, but they too started to break after Sullivan's collapse. By eleven o'clock only a Maryland regiment and a Delaware regiment still stood fast. By this time Grant's men were attacking from the front, the Hessians from the east and the van of the column from the Jamaica pass was approaching from the rear. The only escape route lay westward through the swamps, so Sullivan dispatched as many as he could in this direction along any path they could find. After this, he resolutely led 250 of his Marylanders against the British blocking his rear, with the intention of cutting his own way back to the Brooklyn defences and at the same time protecting the men already on their way to safety. Five times the Marylanders charged; five times they came stumbling back. Washington, watching from his vantage point in the rear, is said to have exclaimed: 'Good God, what brave fellows I must lose this day!' Many of the early leavers did manage to flounder across the marshes and reach the safety of the Brooklyn defences. Joseph Plumb Martin, a sixteen-year-old from Massachusetts, was with the reserve and described how he saw them struggling out of the swamp. 'When they came out of the water and mud towards us,' he said, 'they looked like water-rats; it was truly a pitiful sight.' But the escape of the main body was at the expense of the gallant rearguard. Their task achieved the Marylanders attempted to fight their own way to safety. Only one officer and nine men achieved it. The rest were killed, drowned or captured. Stirling himself was made a prisoner.

*

By noon the British had won a great victory and were in possession of the field. The engagement was a serious disaster for the Americans as they lost about 1,500 men killed, wounded or captured, while the British losses totalled only 370. After the battle the British pressed on towards the Brooklyn lines. Howe was now in some doubt as to what to do. His troops hoped an immediate assault would be ordered, but, remembering the losses suffered when storming Breed's Hill the year before, Howe decided to wait and make a formal siege approach on the lines as soon as the guns of the fleet were able to come to his aid.

Washington was also hesitant. At first he decided to reinforce the troops he already had in the Brooklyn defences, and fight it out; then, after a trying night spent waiting for the British to attack, he had second thoughts. On the afternoon of 29 August, two days after his defeat on the Long Island Heights, he assembled his generals for a council of war, ostensibly to obtain their views on a course of action, actually to tell him of his decision to evacuate the Brooklyn lines.

Washington made careful plans to get his men safely back across the East River to Manhattan. To hold the position after the other units had withdrawn and to cover the embarkation he selected five proven regiments. In command he placed Thomas Mifflin, a young brigadier who had earlier been on his staff.[1] Next, a huge miscellaneous assortment of craft from all the creeks around Manhattan were assembled on the New York side. To man the boats, seamen were taken from the Marblehead 14th Continentals and from the 27th Continentals who came from New England fishing ports.

The evacuation began at dusk and, thanks to Washington's careful preparations, went very smoothly, with a blanket of fog conveniently deadening the sounds of departure. Silently and with as much speed as could be mustered in the foggy darkness, the troops filed into the waiting boats. Then the New England seamen took them into the darkness of the East River, navigating to start with in the strong current of an ebb tide. They went without lights in a fog that obscured the lines of the New York shore. When they heard the sound of oarlocks they had no way of knowing whether the nearby boat was a British craft or one of their own. Unerringly through the night they put boatload after boatload of Continentals ashore on Manhattan's piers, and then went back for more. Just after midnight it seemed as if the evacuation could not be finished in time, for the wind changed and the necessary additional sailing craft could no longer be taken into the broad reaches. However, after a short period of anxiety the wind shifted again and sailing craft could be employed once more. There were mistakes. Sometimes men piled up at the ferry slipway

[1] And was later to become his troublesome Quartermaster General.

in alarming confusion. The worst incident occurred at two o'clock in the morning when Mifflin in charge of the rearguard was told by an aide that the boats were ready to take off his men. He immediately ordered them out of the trenches and down to the slipway; but when they arrived, long lines of troops were found waiting for boats. Washington close to despair rode up and exclaimed angrily: 'Good God, General Mifflin! You have ruined us by withdrawing your troops from the line.' Explaining briefly how the mistake had occurred, Mifflin ordered his units back to the trenches. That they went was a tribute to their courage and discipline—and the care in their selection by Washington.

Just as dawn was breaking, Mifflin's men were able to leave. Fortunately the fog that blanketed the river and the shores during the night now rolled in thicker than ever. Though the British had already begun to realise that the Americans were uncannily quiet, they could not see what was going on. When patrols eventually probed forward it was to discover that the Brooklyn lines had been abandoned.

One of the last to leave was Lieutenant Tallmadge of the rearguard's Connecticut battalion under Colonel Chester. Tallmadge describes his departure as follows. 'As the dawn of the day approached those of us who remained in the trenches became very anxious for our own safety, and when dawn appeared there were several regiments still on duty. At this time a very dense fog began to rise and it seemed to settle in a peculiar manner over both encampments . . . so very dense was the atmosphere that I could scarcely discern a man at six yards distance . . . When we reached the Brooklyn ferry, the boats had not returned from their last trip, but they very soon appeared and took the whole regiment over to New York. I think I saw General Washington on the ferry stairs when I stepped into one of the last boats that received the troops. I left my horse tied to a post at the ferry.' But that was not the end of the matter. Once ashore in New York, Tallmadge seems to have had second thoughts about leaving his favourite horse tied up at a pier in Brooklyn. The fog was thicker than ever, and the lieutenant sought permission to take some volunteers in a flat-bottomed boat to fetch the animal. Presumably Colonel Chester agreed, for Tallmadge and some soldiers went back across the river. They got the horse aboard and were well out into the East River's current when British soldiers appeared on the quay behind them. They were peppered by musketry, and by a few light field pieces that were wheeled on to the pier, but they rowed back unharmed to Manhattan. Thus although most sources say that not a shot was fired, young Tallmadge evidently received an official British farewell from Long Island.

[2]

After their defeat of the Americans on Long Island the British hoped that the rebels might be more ready to come to terms, and they made another attempt at conciliation; but when their approach brought no response preparations were made for the invasion of Manhattan.

*

Washington, meanwhile, was finding it extremely difficult to decide what to do. The advice of General Greene was to burn the town. 'Two-thirds belong to the Tories,' he said, 'so we have no great reason to run any risk for its defence and burning it will deprive the enemy of an opportunity of barracking the whole army together.' Congress, however, would not allow the destruction of New York and told Washington it must be held 'at every hazard'. In his customary way Washington called a series of councils of war, and by the time the second was sitting, having warned Congress that holding New York would probably entail the destruction of the army, he had received permission to proceed as he thought best. With this sanction Washington and his colleagues decided to evacuate New York as soon as the arms and equipment stored there had been moved; but in the event the British invasion began before the task was completed. To meet the British attack there were Putnam's 5,000 men in New York itself, Greene's division of a similar size spread along the Manhattan shore from New York to Harlem, and Heath's force of some 9,000 which held bridgeheads on either side of the Harlem River in the north.

*

The first British move was to sail up the East River and occupy the islands off Harlem. Because of this Washington, not unnaturally, expected the attack to be made in the north. When it was launched from Newtown Creek between Brooklyn and Queens against the middle of Greene's[1] line he was caught completely by surprise. In fact, Howe had originally intended to land at Harlem, but the waters in that area were so treacherous that frigates could not approach the shore, and rather than land without naval support Howe changed his objective to Kip's Bay opposite Newtown Creek. It was a fortunate decision. The men guarding Kip's Bay were the rawest of recruits, some of whom had been in the army less

---

[1] Greene was absent sick at the start of the operation and Spencer was in charge.

Admiral Lord Howe by H. Singleton

than a week. The better regiments were farther south and, quite fortuitously, the invaders arrived where the greenest soldiers had been posted. Also, as a matter of routine only half were present and they had been on duty all night and had not yet received the day's rations. All in all, the Kip's Bay defences were in a sorry condition.

During the night five British warships moved into the cove. The Americans heard them drop anchor, and during the hours of darkness exchanged bantering insults with the British sailors aboard. At daybreak it appeared the ships had not come merely for conversation. They were anchored bow to stern in a line parallel to the shore, and their cannon had been run out through the gun ports. The five frigates looked alarmingly powerful. Their masts and rigging towered in the air; their black hulls check-banded with white were bristling with guns. At about ten o'clock a flotilla of flatboats loaded with soldiers assembled off Newtown Creek. On the incoming tide the boats advanced, with the soldiers standing in ranks, their muskets on their shoulders. In their brilliant scarlet and white they made a splendid, frightening sight which completely demoralised the Americans in the shallow trenches around Kip's Bay. But before the militia could react to the invaders the sailors in front of them sprang into action. The start of the assault boats across the water had been the signal to loose their broadsides. Shortly before eleven the entire line opened fire. Cannon balls soared over the trenches; dust, smoke and sods of earth filled the air. Joseph Martin had been wiling away the time studying old papers in a shed behind the trenches. He was so scared, he relates, that without realising what he was doing he took an enormous frog-leap back into his trench.

The ships' gunners saw their enemy well enough, but could not depress their pieces below the horizontal, so most of the missiles whistled over the Americans' heads. But, although almost nobody was hit, the shock was sufficient. The Connecticut recruits immediately started to break and run. First, they abandoned their trenches and fled to the cover of the wood at the edge of the meadow. Then, they moved back to the post road which joined New York to Harlem and 'hot-footed' it towards Heath's force on the Harlem Heights. The panic which started in Kip's Bay then spread up and down the whole line. By the time the assault boats reached the warships—at which moment the bombardment ceased—only the brigade commander and a handful of men remained in the trenches.

*

The British force of 4,000 included Hessians and footguards but in accordance with custom was composed mainly of grenadier and light infantry companies. As the invaders fanned out to consolidate the bridgehead, the light companies took the right, the Hessians the left, and the grenadier companies and foot guards under General Cornwallis the centre. Meeting only very slight opposition they pushed inland about a mile, crossed the post road, and occupied Inclenberg Hill on which was situated a comfortable country house with its gardens, orchards and fields belonging to the Quaker merchant Robert Murray.

*

The sound of the firing at Kip's Bay, which could be heard clearly in New York, warned Putnam that the invasion had begun; and he reacted immediately. First, he sent off two of his brigades 'to reinforce wherever reinforcing was needed'. Then, he rode north to find out from Washington what he should do.

Putnam was told to get out of New York before the trap closed, and on his return he drew up a bold plan of escape. He decided to try and rush his troops up the west side of the island, keeping as far as possible from the British beachhead. With this in mind, the men were told to leave their work on the evacuation of stores and prepare as quickly as possible for the twelve mile march north.

Though useless as a tactician—as had been seen on Long Island—Putnam possessed energy and enterprise when it came to leading personally in the field. As soon as the head of the column of his 3,000 marchers had set off along the Greenwich road beside the Hudson, he and his aides, one of whom was the notorious Aaron Burr, dashed about on horseback, rounding up stragglers and directing them to the main body. Later, he raced up and down the column shouting encouragement and urging his men to maintain the pace. It was difficult to get them to march fast, for it was a very hot afternoon, but Putnam was certain that only speed could save them.

At the invitation of Mrs. Murray, Howe and his officers took refreshment at the Murray home on Inclenberg Hill. There is a legend that despite her husband's sympathy for the British cause, Mrs. Murray was a patriot, and that she gave the party in order to delay Howe and give Putnam's escapees a chance of getting clear. There may or may not be any truth in this story, but Howe certainly sent no troops from the beachhead across to the west side. Putnam, who was fully expecting to run into a British road-block at any point north of Greenwich, met up with no enemy at all on the march north. Approaching Inclenberg Hill he took the Bloomingdale road which forked left off the post road, and his column got past the British unseen and unopposed.

*

Meanwhile, Washington and his aides were riding towards the sound of the guns. After galloping down the post road, they reached a crossroad short of Inclenberg Hill where they encountered the rabble of men from Kip's Bay in full flight. The sight of his soldiers running away profoundly shocked Washington, and he ordered his aides to try and halt them. The officers waved their swords, shouted curses and did their best to ride herd and stop the stampede. The disorderly retreat, however, had gained too much momentum. When the officers put themselves in the way, the militiamen swept round and, abandoning the road, took to the fields.

Returning to the crossroad, Washington next encountered the two brigades sent by Putnam. They had arrived in good order up the Bloomingdale road and were halted, the leading brigade in the crossroad leading to the post road and the other still on the Bloomingdale road. Washington believed it was not too late to make a stand. He saw, too, that the stone walls along the crossroad would make a good place to set up a battle line. He therefore ordered the commanders of Putnam's brigades to march their men forward and take up a defensive position. But it was not to be. As the word was passed along the halted columns, the discipline of the march up from the south suddenly collapsed. The men had been watching the Kip's Bay brigades 'hot-footing' it to the north. They became infected with the same disease. Paying not the least attention to the commands of their officers, they began dashing out of the ranks and running off across country; and what had been a potent holding force quickly degenerated into a formless unmanageable mob. In a desperate attempt to stop them, Washington rode down the disintegrating columns and tried to get some at least to stand and fight.

'Take the wall! Take the cornfield!' he shouted angrily, pointing to positions along the crossroad.

The response was poor. Most of the men ignored his orders completely. A few got in place behind the walls, but, as soon as he moved on, slipped off back across the road to join their comrades fleeing north.

About this time British soldiers appeared on the crest of Inclenberg Hill, and the sight of them completed the rout. Realising at last that his men were incapable of making a fight of it, Washington now lost the last vestiges of his self-control. He tore off his hat and dashed it to the ground. Cursing violently, he roared out that they were not men but scum, and it was impossible to fight a war with cowards for soldiers. In his fury he slashed at them with his whip and tried to beat courage into them. But his frenzy, formidable though it was, accomplished nothing. The men continued to break away, and finally Washington and his aides were left alone amid a litter of equipment thrown aside to make running easier. Meanwhile, the British detachment was descending the hill and coming in their direction. There seemed a real danger that the general might be killed or captured, for he sat dejectedly on his mount, his head bowed, making no attempt to move. Finally, the British soldiers having approached almost within musket range, one of his aides, plucking up courage, grasped firmly the bridle of the dazed general's horse and led him away to safety.

*

In the evening, when the British beachhead had been consolidated, Howe, having sent a detachment of Hessians to occupy New York, marched off the rest of his army in the wake of the American fugitives. Rather strangely, while the British column was moving up the post road, the last units of Putnam's force were marching up the Bloomingdale road a mile or so to the west, on parallel lines, and in the same direction. But the two forces never contacted one another.

During the late afternoon and evening Washington attempted to reorganise his stricken army. Of his 16,000 men he placed 6,000 on the far side of the Harlem River to protect King's Bridge against a turning movement, and with the remainder he manned the Harlem Heights in a triple line stretching from the Harlem River in the east to the Hudson in the west. After the fiasco of Kip's Bay, he doubted if his men would stand and fight; but he gave them the advantage that the high ground offered and hoped for the best.

Shortly before dawn next day, 16 September 1776, some rangers under Colonel Knowlton while on reconnaissance in the valley between the opposing forces brushed with a British detachment. Knowlton hastily withdrew and was reporting to Washington and the Adjutant General Reed when from across the valley was heard the derisory hunting call of 'Gone to Ground'. To Washington and Reed who were both foxhunting men the sound of the loud swelling notes alternating with quiet tremolos was a supreme insult, so they hastily planned a counter-attack. The result was that Knowlton's rangers, reinforced by some Virginians under Major Leitch, were started off back across the valley to try and get behind the British force, while the rest of the Virginia regiment staged a feint frontal attack.

The entry of royal troops in New York

The frontal attack did all it should have done to hold the enemy's attention. The enveloping force, however, came into action too soon and both Knowlton and Leitch were mortally wounded. Not to be outdone, Washington then reinforced the enveloping force, and it managed to drive back the enemy, who retired first to the high ground south of the valley, and then to their main front line.

After the second British withdrawal, Washington called off the engagement, which, although its tactical results were nil, because the redcoats had retired, had raised American morale from the depths to which it had fallen. Reed[1] in a letter to his wife went so far as to say: 'You can hardly conceive the change it has made in our army. The men have recovered their spirits and feel a confidence which before they had quite lost. I hope the effects will be lasting.' In the event Reed's hopes were not fulfilled. Plundering and desertion by the militia continued and their bad example was soon followed by the Continentals. The state of the army seemed to Washington deplorable and his task as commander almost impossible. On 22 September, he wrote[2] woefully to his brother John Augustine: 'It is not in the power of words to describe the task I have to act . . . fifty thousand pounds should not induce me again to undergo what I have done.'

In the lull following the battle, Washington wrote to Congress suggesting how the army might be improved. He asked particularly for a long-term army to be embodied so that the use of the militia might be obviated. He also suggested that the Articles of War be strengthened to improve discipline. His recommendations were eventually carried out, but not in time to improve the immediate situation.

*

Several weeks now passed while the cautious Howe prepared his next move; and there was then a further delay when attention had to be given to a fire in New York which raged for two days. This destroyed about a quarter of the city but left sufficient accommodation intact to provide winter quarters for the invaders.

Finally, on 12 October, Howe began the operation that Washington had long feared. He despatched by sea 4,000 troops under Cornwallis up East River, through the treacherous racing waters of Hell Gate and past the mouth of the Bronx, with the object of landing at Throg's Point and attacking the Americans guarding King's Bridge from the east.

[1] 1 Reed 238.
[2] 6 G.W. 96.

Throg's Point proved an unfortunate choice as a landing place. Although shown on maps as a peninsula it was a marshy island separated from the mainland by a dyke whose bridge had been dismantled by the Americans. Realising no advance could be made in this area Cornwallis re-embarked his troops and landed them again at Pell's Point half a mile farther north. The second landing was unopposed, but on advancing inland the British were held up by a detachment of New Englanders under Colonel Glover.

*

In answer to the threats in the east, Washington redeployed his forces. First he evacuated Manhattan except for some 2,000 men who were left in Fort Washington on the northern tip of the island. Next, he sent 3,000 men across the Hudson to Fort Lee on the New Jersey side and placed the two fortresses under the command of Greene who had now fully re-covered from his illness. These moves conformed with a resolution of Congress that 'the fort and Fort Lee opposite with the obstacles across the Hudson between should be maintained if it be practicable by every art and at whatever expense'. Finally, Washington sent off a brigade to White Plains to oppose the British landings on the east shore and then he led the rest of his army north to a position from which he could reinforce the brigade.

While moving north, Washington was joined by Charles Lee who had just concluded his successful operations in the south, and this led the commander-in-chief to re-organise his forces once again. He split the army into seven divisions commanded by Lee, Greene, Putnam, Heath, Benjamin Lincoln, Spencer and Sullivan.[1] Greene's division was left occupying Fort Washington and Fort Lee, and the remaining 14,500, who were now under Washington's personal command, were placed in position at White Plains, with a defended line of communication back to the Hudson to give an escape route to New Jersey if required. The American position was on a line of hills south of the village of White Plains with the right flank protected by the Bronx River and the left by a millpond. As a second thought, the militia on Chatterton's Hill west of the Bronx River were reinforced by a full brigade of Continentals.

*

It did not take long for Cornwallis to drive back Glover's men at Pell's Point; but in the attack he was slightly wounded. He quickly recovered and then continued to lead his troops vigorously. After occupying New

[1] Captured on Long Island but now exchanged.

General Sir William Howe,
engraving by J. Chapman

Rochelle there was a pause of several days to establish the place as a supply base; then on 23 October, the main body having come up, General Howe led his whole force in a slow five-day advance against Washington's position at White Plains.

Following a reconnaissance, Howe decided that Chatterton's Hill to the west of the Bronx River was the key to the American position, and, after a feint frontal assault to draw the attention of the enemy, he sent a force of 4,000 men across the river to capture the hill. The enveloping force was checked at first by the fire from the defenders on the hill, but having brought cannon into action to soften up the position, it was able to cross the stream and start climbing the frontal slopes. Meanwhile, a force of Hessians crossed the stream farther south and began ascending the western slopes of the hill. The development of the pincer attack on the hill quickly proved too much for its American defenders. The militia fled in panic immediately, and after a brief stand the Continentals followed suit.

The British next move was to haul cannon to the top of the newly captured Chatterton's Hill and from there rake the entire American line from the flank. This second British manoeuvre was as successful as the earlier one had been, for Washington first withdrew his whole line to a prepared position half a mile in the rear, and then, when Howe was seen to have received reinforcements, to a third entrenched position on North Castle Heights.

From then on, however, the British made little use of the advantages gained in the first stages of the battle. Having probed the last American position over the course of several days, Howe came to the conclusion that it was too strong to be successfully stormed by the force at his disposal; and, most surprisingly, he turned his army about and returned to Manhattan.

*

Howe's unexpected withdrawal put Washington in a quandary. For a time he was at his most hesitant. Finally, he came to the conclusion that Howe might either advance up the Hudson to join a British force coming from Canada, or, alternatively, might cross into New Jersey and march towards the capital Philadelphia. With this in mind, he took measures to meet such possible moves by the enemy. To counter an advance north, he left Lee with 7,000 men on the North Castle Heights. To halt a British force from Canada, he despatched to Albany 4,000 men under Heath. Finally, to meet a western move, he led the 2,000 troops that remained, first to Peekskill, and then across the Hudson to join Greene and his men around Fort Lee on the west bank of the river.

Washington's most difficult issue was to decide whether or not to hold Fort Washington. The commander-in-chief's own inclination was not to do so, but Greene was insistent that the place should be held. On 12 November, accompanied by Greene, he had himself rowed over to inspect the fortress. Its commander—Colonel Magraw—also seemed anxious that it should be held, so Washington postponed his decision.

On 15 November Howe's men began attacking the fort from the south whereupon Greene on his own initiative reinforced the garrison. Later on the same day, while at Hackensack four miles away organising an escape route through New Jersey, Washington received a despatch saying that Magraw was being attacked from both north and south, but was 'determined to defend the post or die'. Washington returned to Fort Lee and shortly before dawn on 16 November crossed the Hudson again along with Greene to settle finally what should be done. But they arrived too late. On landing, they learned that enemy troops had breeched the southern defence line and were now assailing the second line. Washington quickly came to the conclusion that his presence was an embarrassment to Magraw who had his hands full, so, restraining an impulse to take personal command, he returned with Greene to Fort Lee.

*

Just before noon it was learned that Cornwallis had brought a column across the Harlem River on the east and the stricken fort was being attacked from three sides. From the ramparts of Fort Lee, Washington and his companions heard the firing growing in volume as the British closed in. By the early afternoon fighting could be seen going on near the river bank, and it was clear that the enemy were within musket range of the inner fort. Washington was now convinced that the place could not be held and sent Magraw instructions to hold on until midnight and then evacuate his men to the Fort Lee side of the river. However, although Greene collected the boats and made the necessary arrangements, it was not to be. First, it was learnt that Magraw was considering seeking terms. Then, the officer with the evacuation order returned with news to depress the stoutest heart: 'Colonel Magraw,' he said, 'sent his thanks to the General but had to report that he had gone so far with negotiations for surrender that he could not in honour break them off.'[1]

*

While still at Fort Lee Washington prepared a candid report for Congress of the sad affair. Then he returned to Hackensack to resume his interrupted efforts to establish a line of retreat for what remained of his army. On 20 November a despatch from Greene told him that a strong British force had crossed the Hudson and was approaching Fort Lee. Washington first confirmed the report and then rode over to organise the evacuation of the fortress. There was only one avenue of escape and that was the line he had been reconnoitring across the Hackensack River. As there was but one bridge the Americans would have to reach it first. To lose a minute was to risk an army—if it could still be styled an army. The drums beat; the men fell in; Washington put himself at the head of the column of 2,000 men; and off they marched. Behind them they left most of the cannon, the tents, the entrenching tools and nearly all the baggage. 'This loss,' wrote Washington, 'was inevitable.' In justice to the quartermasters he added: 'As many of the stores had been removed as circumstances and time would admit of. The ammunition had been happily got away.'[2] It was a high price, but Washington got what he was willing to pay for—access to the bridge over the Hackensack. With a few hours to spare the Americans were able to escape and to make their way to Newark, New Jersey.

[1] 6 G.W. 287.
[2] 6 G.W. 295–298.

Chapter Five

TRENTON AND PRINCETON

'I cannot but remember the place New Jersey holds in the early history of our country. I remember that in the Revolutionary struggle, none had more of its battlefields. I remember reading in my youth a small book— The Life of Washington—and of his struggles none fixed itself in my mind so indelibly as the crossing of the Delaware preceding the battle of Trenton.'

Abraham Lincoln
21 February 1861, State House, Trenton.

The crossing of Cornwallis's division to the west bank of the Hudson suggested that the British were intending to march on Philadelphia, and with this in mind Washington sent an urgent request to Lee at White Plains to come and reinforce him. Lee's 5,000 men would more than double the army, but in a few days the mobile reserve[1] were due for discharge, and Lee's early arrival was vital if there was to be any chance of protecting Philadelphia.

While waiting to see if the British were going to advance, Washington set about trying to get reinforcements from other sources. He sent Reed to ask for help from Governor Livingston of New Jersey. He despatched the eloquent Mifflin on a similar mission to Congress. He also sent a personal request to the same body to forward money to pay the reserve, for he believed that if the men were compensated they might very well re-enlist.

Washington's efforts proved more rewarding than he had dared hope. A thoroughly alarmed Congress authorised the despatch of the New Jersey and Pennsylvania regiments then serving in the Northern Department. They also ruled that the Pennsylvania militia be asked to serve for six weeks more. Finally, they despatched the Philadelphia German battalion and requested Governor Patrick Henry of Virginia to send to his former colleague the Virginia Light Horse.

---

[1] Some 2,000 men of the Maryland and New Jersey contingents of the so-called Flying Camp which had originally been at Amboy.

This was all very helpful. But in spite of several entreating letters there was still no word from Lee. The other reinforcements would take time to arrive, and without Lee's support the American army was not strong enough to give battle. Thus, on 28 November a retreat was ordered from Newark to Brunswick. None too soon as it happened, for the American rearguard left Newark as the British entered on the opposite side of the town.

On 20 November a letter arrived from Lee. It was addressed to Reed and Washington wondered whether he should open it. When, after some qualms, he did break the seal he wished he had left it alone, for it contained some highly unflattering remarks about himself. The letter read:

> I received your most obliging letter—lament with you that fatal indecision of mind which in war is a much greater disqualification than stupidity or want of personal courage. Accident may put a decisive blunderer in the right, but eternal defeat and miscarriage must attend the man of the best parts if cursed with indecision . . .

Washington was not surprised the cocksure Lee should hold such an opinion of him, but was distressed to discover that the seemingly loyal Reed was of the same mind. However, he did not want to lose the services of his valuable assistant,[1] so although he wrote to Reed and explained how he had come to open the letter, he forebore any recrimination and merely thanked him for what he was doing in raising recruits and sent respects to his wife.

*

On 1 December the men discharged went their several ways. Washington was now left with only 3,400 effectives, and he considered it wise to retreat again, this time to Trenton via Princeton where he left Stirling's brigade as a rearguard. He was becoming convinced that he had not time to build up a sufficient force to hold the British on the east of the Delaware and with this in mind set in train plans which were to have an important effect on the course of operations. He ordered the collection and removal of all the boats from the New Jersey bank of the Delaware over a stretch of seventy miles above Philadelphia. Then he crossed with his army into Pennsylvania.

While Washington was at Trenton he received two messages from Lee, both suggesting that it would be better to remain in the north of New Jersey and threaten the rear of the British army rather than join the commander-in-chief. In the second Lee wrote: 'It will be difficult I'm afraid to join you, but cannot I do more service by attacking the British rear?' All

[1] Reed was Adjutant General at the time.

The capture of General Charles Lee

this was quite contrary to what Washington wanted, but he had scarcely time to consider it before he learnt that Lee had been captured. Why this happened has never exactly been determined. Probably it was an amorous adventure that led Lee to spend the night at White's Tavern three miles from the main body of his army. Howe, alarmed to hear of Americans in his rear, sent out a patrol to discover what they were about. Led by Banastre Tarleton it swooped on White's Tavern and took Lee prisoner. But one good result came out of the affair. Although Lee had already allowed a large number of his men to go home because of illness or lack of equipment, there remained some 2,000, and these his second-in-command Sullivan brought speedily to join the commander-in-chief.

*

Meanwhile, Washington decided to strike a blow at the British rather than wait for them to make a move. He drew up a bold scheme whereby a force of 2,400 picked men would cross the Delaware on Christmas night and attack Trenton at dawn from the north. Included in the plan were instructions to Ewing to cross with his militia just south of the town to cut off a retreat, and to Cadwalader to cross farther south to stop reinforcements coming up. There were plenty of craft available thanks to Washington's foresight in collecting the vessels on the Pennsylvania bank. Most were Durham boats capable of carrying fifteen tons. These were used in normal times to transport ore on the river. They were rowed downstream with eighteen-foot sweeps and had walking rails for poling upstream.

Washington assembled his chosen Continental regiments on Christmas afternoon in a sheltered valley a mile west of McKonkey's Ferry; and to inspire them to do their best read out to them the words of a stirring pamphlet produced by Thomas Paine, whose most spirited lines were: 'The summer soldier and sunshine patriot will in this crisis shrink from the service of their country; but he that stands it now deserves the love and thanks of man and woman. Up and help us; lay your shoulder to the wheel; the heart that feels not now is dead.'

Washington took with him three times the normal ratio of artillery to infantry. This was wise, bearing in mind the sleet, for cannon was capable of being used in bad weather as its vital touch-hole powder could be protected more easily than the powder in a musket's pan.

Because of the importance of the artillery, the infantry was subordinated to its passage, and Knox's[1] great booming voice was used to marshal the whole force for the difficult crossing of the ice-choked river. But the loading of eighteen cannon and their draft horses took longer than had been expected. By midnight Washington had hoped to have all his men and guns across, only to find everything three hours behind schedule. Then, even when the crossing was completed, another hour passed while the troops marched to their starting points within the arc of Stephen's advanced brigade.

A light snowfall had covered the ground by the time they started off, and the wind had risen during the crossing and was roaring angrily. Now with the approach of dawn snow began to fall again. Mingled with it was rain that froze and glazed the road. More difficult conditions for a march could hardly have been encountered.

Leading the column down the slippery road towards Trenton was Stephen's brigade with forty scouts ahead. Next came Greene's division with Mercer's brigade in front and Stirling's following. Four cannon were at the head of Mercer's men and three preceded Stirling's. Marching in the rear with two more cannon was Fermoy's brigade. This had the

[1] Washington's chief of artillery.

Leutze's inaccurate, but dramatic, portrayal of Washington crossing the Delaware (courtesy of the Metropolitan Museum of Art, gift of John S. Kennedy, 1897)

task of moving later to the east to secure the road to Princeton. At first, Sullivan's division followed Greene's, but on arrival at the road junction east of Howell's Ferry, Greene took first Scotch road and then Pennington road while Sullivan followed the parallel river road.

Washington was with Greene's column, and two miles short of Trenton, as it came to a halt, he rode forward to discover the reason. Looking up a side road he saw in the half light a group of men crouching by a wood. When he asked about them, he was told they were Americans sent out by Stephen the day before to try and locate the enemy's outposts. Earlier they had found a post on the road ahead and shot a sentry who had not seen them approaching because of the raging storm. Stephen was standing nearby while this report was being made, and Washington turned on him in a fury. How had he dared to send a patrol across the river on the day before the expedition started. 'You, sir,' exclaimed Washington, 'may have ruined all my plans by having put the enemy on their guard!' However, it was no good wasting any more time. The damage had been done. Washington, therefore, gave the order for the advance to continue.

About eight o'clock Greene's leading troops reached the Pennington road, and having passed through some woods came to a point about half a mile from Trenton. Ahead was the picket post where the German sentry had been shot by Stephen's men, and as they approached a challenge rang out. Then came shouts and words of command, and a score of Hessians emerged from the building. Although at extreme range the Americans opened fire. The Hessians replied, but after their volley had gone wide in the roaring storm, they made off hurriedly across the fields towards Trenton.

*

When the British advanced forces had reached the Delaware, Howe halted them while he completed his plans for the winter. Eventually, he despatched Clinton with a force of 6,000 by sea to Rhode Island to establish a base for a New England operation in the following year, but left his remaining 23,000 men in winter quarters with his options open. Based on New York, about half were east of the Hudson and the rest scattered across New Jersey. The troops nearest Washington were the 3,000 men of the Hessian division under General von Donop stationed in Mount Holly, Burlington, Bordontown and Trenton, all to the east of the Delaware; and it was the three regiments commanded by Colonel Rall in Trenton who were the object of Washington's attack.

Contrary to some accounts, the Hessians appear to have celebrated

Christmas in Trenton in a seemly manner.[1] They set up Christmas trees in their quarters, exchanged gifts, and attended the divine services arranged by their chaplains. There was plenty of room for them in the town as most of the inhabitants had abandoned their homes.

Colonel Rall was first alerted after the enemy patrol had shot the sentry at the post on the Pennington road on Christmas night. Fearing this might be the prelude to a serious attack, he rode out at the head of his twenty attached British dragoons to investigate. The party went up the high street and took the Pennington road. They passed the post, where all was now quiet, and went on up Scotch road. Although they heard noises in the woods they could not find any enemy, and, having given orders for the post to be strengthened, Rall returned with his troopers to the town.

The second alert was when Greene's men in Washington's presence fired on the same post early on Christmas morning. It came just as the old guard was being dismissed and the new guard was being mounted, so that the details who were from Rall's own regiment were able to form up quickly at their battle stations. Meanwhile, the rest of the regiment marched up from the lower part of the town and assembled in the churchyard opposite Rall's headquarters in the high street, and they were joined by the Lössing regiment from the upper part of the town. At the same time, the Knyphausen regiment moved across from the area of the old barracks by the river and formed up outside the Quaker meeting house in the south-east. Although the troops were quickly in position, Rall himself was hard to rouse. It was difficult at first to convince him that it was any more serious than the first alarm had been and by the time he had appeared and mounted his horse to take charge, the Americans were already in the outskirts of the town.

*

The battle began with American cannon coming into action and firing down the high street and the parallel Bridge street which led to the Assunpink Creek in the south. Two Hessian cannon were manhandled into position outside Rall's headquarters to reply, but after one shot had been fired and fell short, the horses were hitched in and the pieces moved up the street to a better position. In the artillery duel that followed the Americans did better than the Hessians who only managed to fire twelve times including their parting salvo. Then, on trying to retire, five of the eight draft horses were shot and the two cannon had to be abandoned. A

[1] According to Smith, p. 17, there is no on-the-scene evidence of widespread drinking in British, American *or* German camps.

number of the artillerymen were also killed or wounded from the small arms fire of the men of Mercer's brigade who had moved down into houses on the west side of the high street.

After successfully driving back the artillerymen, the Americans opened fire on the Hessians assembled in the churchyard. Rall's first reaction was to retreat to the shelter of the orchard to the east, but when he found Fermoy's brigade blocking his way, he returned. He next planned to attack the Americans and try and drive them from the town. Owing to a mistaken order, the Knyphausen regiment never joined in, and the Rall and Lössing regiments on their own proved too weak for the task. Advancing in a snowstorm, the two regiments were fired at on their right flank by the American cannon at the top of the town, and in front met the withering fire of Mercer's men reinforced now by some of Stirling's brigade. The Hessians advanced gallantly, but suffered severely, and when Rall was mortally wounded they began to lose heart. Then Fermoy's men came charging in from the rear shouting at them to surrender, and the poor harassed Germans started to lay down their arms and capitulate.

The men of the Knyphausen regiment by the Quaker meeting-house could see across the fields their comrades surrendering. They could also see Americans entering the town by the river road and moving round to seize the bridge over the Assunpink and close the southern escape route. Judging the situation hopeless, the majority decided to give themselves up, and moved off to do so, but a number including several officers attempted to swim across the Assunpink, and fifty of these got safely away. The sergeant in charge of the detachment guarding the bridge recorded later that 650 out of the 1,586 in Trenton escaped. The first to cross, he said, were the twenty dragoons. Then came Jaegers from the river road post followed by the musicians of the band and a few stragglers. The men of the Knyphausen regiment who swam to safety appear afterwards to have lost their way, and, according to one report, to have 'suffered incredible fatigue'; but they were the first to reach Princeton and inform General Leslie of the capture of Trenton. One of the officers was given a horse and sent to Brunswick to tell General Grant what had happened, and Grant in his turn sent the same escapee to New York to report to General Howe.

*

The Americans captured in Trenton a quantity of ammunition, several stands of small arms and six cannon; but the booty was not as great as Washington had expected, and he was now in a difficult position. Von

Donop would undoubtedly be alerted by the escapees from Trenton, and soon several enemy forces might be converging on him. Also, he was without the support of Ewing and Cadwalader, both of whom had failed to carry out their missions. Bearing all this in mind he decided to go back across the Delaware.

The return journey proved almost as difficult as the march out had been. Herding prisoners, and accompanied by several wagon loads of booty, the Americans set out for the ferry in the teeth of a wintry storm. Then the crossing through the ice floes was even more bitter than before and three men were frozen to death. The troops did not begin to reach their old bivouacks until late in the afternoon and by then were almost completely exhausted by the battle and the long marches to and from Trenton; but they were nevertheless quite happy, for they had tasted victory after many months of continuous defeat.

*

After Ewing had taken a look at the river on Christmas night he had considered it impassable, and assuming Washington would come to the same conclusion, he marched his men back to camp. Cadwalader sent some of his men across, but after deciding that it would be impossible to take the artillery and the horses over the turbulent waters, he recalled those on the other side and returned to camp also. Ewing seems to have done no more in the matter, but Cadwalader wrote to Washington to explain his failure and said he imagined the badness of the night must have also prevented the main army crossing. Later, when he came to realise that he had been penning his letter at the very time that Washington's men were fighting their way into Trenton he was stung into action. Without even telling the commander-in-chief, he took his whole force across the river. The passage which took place on 27 December was no easier than it would have been on the 25th, but now they knew it could be done nothing could stop Cadwalader and his men. They pushed straight ahead and soon discovered that not only had the Hessian garrison in Bordontown been withdrawn but that Trenton itself had not been reoccupied. On finding out this, a message was sent to Washington inviting him to join them.

Cadwalader's bold move placed Washington in a difficult position again. A number of his men were due to be discharged. They might very well refuse to re-enlist just when the operation was in progress. Also, even if they agreed to serve on he would still have only a very small force to oppose the sort of effort an indignant and powerful enemy would be likely to make to avenge the humiliating defeat at Trenton. On the other

he surrender of the Hessians at Trenton by John Trumbull

hand, Washington knew that if he ordered his subordinate to return it might be considered an ignominious retreat on the heels of a brilliant victory. After some hesitation therefore he finally decided to join Cadwalader. On 29 December he crossed the Delaware again.

*

One of Washington's first tasks after reoccupying Trenton was to visit his regiments, personally to urge the men whose time has expired to re-enlist. An offer of a $10 bounty coupled with a plea of patriotism brought unexpectedly good results. More than half of them, buoyed by the late victory, agreed to serve for six weeks longer.

Thus, by the evening of 31 December, Washington found himself with a hard core of 1,600 veterans which with Cadwalader's contingent and Mifflin's militia who were on their way from Philadelphia. would give him a force of some 5,000 men. He was sufficiently satisfied to decide to fight but before doing so, and while waiting for Mifflin's troops to arrive, he sent out his cavalry in the direction of Princeton to find out something of the enemy's dispositions. The reconnaissance party discovered that Princeton was strongly held, and after skilfully skirmishing with some British dragoons brought back two troopers as prisoners. From these it was learnt that Cornwallis had joined Grant at Princeton with 8,000 reinforcements; but Washington still boldly resolved to stand and fight, though he decided not to do so at Trenton, and hurriedly sought an alternative position. After a careful appreciation of the situation, he despatched Fermoy's brigade to slow the British advance from Princeton, and withdrew the rest of his force to the ridge along the south bank of Assunpink Creek.

It was a good defensive position although there were a number of fords that the British might attempt to use as well as the bridge beside the millpond. Hitchcock was given the task of guarding the ford to the south of the high street, St. Clair covered the bridge and the nearby Millham Ford, Cadwalader was to watch the crossing by Henry's mill, and Mercer was responsible for the right flank. Finally, as it seemed likely that the engagement would take the form of a rearguard action, only a small proportion of the forty cannon[1] were brought into action.

While Washington was getting ready to defend Assunpink Creek, Fermoy's brigade along with two of Forrest's guns had moved north to try and delay the enemy. By 1 January 1777, Fermoy's force was blocking

---

[1] Two guns of the Philadelphia Association, four of Forrest's battery, a naval gun, and two from the Massachusetts battery.

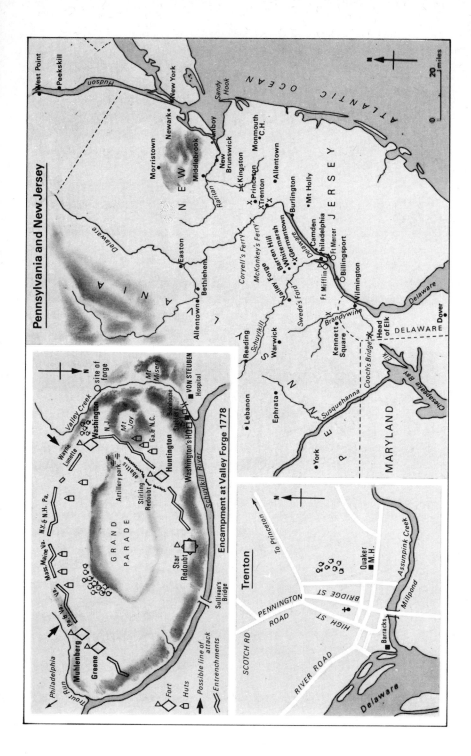

Pennsylvania and New Jersey

West Point
Peekskill
Hudson
New York
Sandy Hook
ATLANTIC OCEAN
20 miles

Newark
Morristown
Middlebrook
Amboy
New Brunswick
Monmouth C.H.
Kingston
Princeton
Trenton
Allentown

N E W   J E R S E Y

Raritan

Easton
Bethlehem
Allentown
Delaware

Corvell's Ferry
McKonkey's Ferry
Valley Forge
Burlington
Mt. Holly
Camden
Philadelphia
Germantown
Ft Mercer
Billingsport
Whitemarsh
Barren Hill

P E N N S Y L V A N I A

Swede's Ford
Ft Mifflin
Wilmington
Delaware

Reading
Schuylkill
Warwick
Brandywine
Kennett Square
Cooch's Bridge
Head of Elk

Lebanon
Ephrata
Susquehanna
Chesapeake Bay

York

MARYLAND
DELAWARE
Dover

Encampment at Valley Forge 1778

N
site of forge
Valley Creek
Mt Misery
Mt Joy
Washington
Wayne
Lunette
Lafayette
N.J.
Ga. & N.C.
Huntington
Bakehouse
Stocker
Washington's HQ
VON STEUBEN
Hospital
Schuylkill River

N.Y. & N.H.
Mass.-Maine
Artillery park
Stirling Redoubt
Va.
Pa.
abattis

G R A N D
P A R A D E

Philadelphia
Muhlenberg
Greene
Pa. & Va.
Trout Run

Sullivan's Bridge
Star Redoubt

Fort △
Huts ⬒
Entrenchments ⩘
Possible line of attack ➡

Trenton

N
To Princeton
PENNINGTON ROAD
SCOTCH RD
Quaker M.H.
Assunpink Creek
BRIDGE ST
HIGH ST
Millpond
Barracks
RIVER ROAD
Delaware

the Princeton road south of Maidenhead. After this, however, Fermoy who was proving a worthless commander for all his European reputation, returned to Trenton in such haste as to raise serious doubts as to his courage, and Hand of the Pennsylvania regiment took over command. Meanwhile, Cornwallis having completed his preparations for recapturing Trenton, and having left three regiments to hold Princeton, was advancing along the Trenton road. At Maidenhead he left three more regiments to protect his line of communications and then set off southward with his remaining 5,500 men and twenty-eight guns. A combination of heavy rain and milder weather had thawed out the ground and the mud bogged down the wheeled vehicles and greatly slowed the advance so that it was not until ten o'clock in the morning that Cornwallis's advanced troops contacted the American delaying force. There followed a morning of vicious little skirmishes during which, disputing each step of the way, Hand's men dropped slowly back. By noon they were behind Shabbakonk Creek where it crosses the Princeton road two miles from Trenton. From under the cover of thick woods they opened fire and halted the enemy in their tracks, compelling the commander of the leading troops to deploy and bring cannon into action, and holding up the advance for three hours. It was not until yet more regiments had been deployed and further cannon used that Hand's men fell back, this time to a ravine of a tributary of the Assunpink a mile from Trenton. While manning the ravine the defenders were visited by Washington and Greene who had ridden forward to encourage them to hold on for as long as possible.

It was not until five o'clock on the wintry evening of 2 January that the British troops eventually reached Trenton; but late though it was, they were sent in immediately against the American prepared position on the south bank of Assunpink Creek. One column went straight down the high street and tried to force their way through the ford at its end. Another attempted to storm the bridge. Neither was successful. The high street column was stopped by withering fire from Hitchcock's men. Those charging the bridge were halted in their tracks by a furious cannonade from Washington's artillery. Three times they charged. Three times they were compelled to withdraw. At nightfall Cornwallis called off the attack. But he was not unduly dismayed at his failure to drive the Americans from their position. They appeared boxed in on all sides[1] and it was only a matter of time, he concluded, before they must surrender.

---

[1] By the Assunpink in the north, the Delaware on the west and the sea on the southeast.

However, rather than stage another attack in the darkness, which might be difficult to carry out, he decided to wait until the morning to finish the matter. Using the hunting metaphor popular with both sides he declared to his officers: 'We've got the old fox safe now. We'll go over and bag him in the morning.'

*

Although Washington had gained a respite, he realised that when daylight came and the enemy chose to attack he would be no match for his foe. A retreat south was a possibility; but it might get him boxed in again. He preferred a move in the opposite direction which would give a better chance of escaping from Cornwallis's clutches and might at the same time offer the opportunity of raiding Princeton. With this in mind he called a council-of-war in a small frame house beside the road to the bridge, and consulted his principal officers. Their decision was unanimous. The army should decamp by night and make a forced march to Princeton around the flank of the enemy.

It was a bold plan, and for its success secrecy was essential, so camp fires were left burning and kept well stoked up, shovels being noisily used in the process; and two howitzers were left in action to fire at intervals during the night. Then, the few men left having been told to scamper off after the army had departed, the rest, led by two Trenton folk who knew every inch of the way, quietly took the road to Princeton. Fortunately the weather had changed. The mud that had impeded Cornwallis was now frozen and the surface of the road was hard. With the wheels of their vehicles muffled with rags and rope the Americans were able to get well away before the British realised they had gone.

*

Washington's army reached the Quaker bridge over the Assunpink two miles east of Maidenhead at about 2 a.m. on the morning of 3 January 1777. As the men plodded along in the darkness, imagination at one point fashioned foes. The cry was raised that the column was surrounded and a few frightened militiamen ran off, but except for this, the march was without incident. As dawn was breaking they approached the stream named Stony Brook which encircles Princeton protectively, and just as the column began to cross, the sun rose. Ahead, a road to the right led to Princeton. Directly in front was a track towards the Quaker meeting house. To the left another road followed Stony Brook to Worth's mill and the bridge where the post road from Princeton to Trenton crossed the stream.

Washington's plan was to attack the British base at Princeton with the bulk of his force while Mercer took 350 men along the road by Stony Brook and destroyed the post road bridge to prevent British reinforcements returning to help their comrades. Shortly before eight o'clock, therefore, Sullivan's division filed off to the right along the road towards Princeton while Mercer and his men set off for the bridge. Then came the unexpected news that an enemy column which had earlier left for Trenton had turned about, recrossed the bridge, and was on its way back towards Princeton. When Mercer saw the British returning along the post road, he ordered his men off to the right across the fields and placed them in position in an orchard on a hill from where enemy movements could be watched. Before the Americans were all under cover the redcoats opened fire, whereupon Mercer changed front and advanced towards them. In the first brush, the Americans had the advantage and drove the British back behind a ragged hedge. In true martial manner as they saw it, Mercer and his officers then began dressing their men in ranks before resuming the advance. The British were close enough to hear the Americans giving their orders, and bawled out in derision: 'Damn you! We'll dress you!' Mercer answered with a smart volley of small arms and cannon fire, and the British having brought all their force into action, a brisk little encounter resulted.

Washington back at the Quaker meeting house, hearing the challenging musketry and answering volleys, rode forward to investigate; and then deciding that Mercer was likely to be driven back, he sent for the next unit on the road which was Cadwalader's Pennsylvania militia. Before the militia came up, the British charged. Mercer's men stood their ground at first, but when the enemy came at them with the bayonet, and Mercer fell mortally wounded, they broke in disorder and ran back towards the Quaker meeting house. The situation was saved temporarily when two American guns on the right opened fire on the British flank. This caused the attackers first to halt and then pull back. The respite, however, was short-lived. Although shaken by the sight of the fleeing Continentals, the militia at first moved forward towards the enemy position. When they were met by a concentrated volley, however, it was too much for them and they took to their heels.

Washington brought up Hitchcock's men in an attempt to retrieve the situation. Then he rode in among the militia and exhorted them to rally alongside the New Englanders. Being out of range, the militia were somewhat recovered from their fright, and began to take heed of what was being said. As soon as a relatively firm line had been formed, Washington placed himself in front and ordered an advance. Steadily the Americans approached the redcoats. At thirty yards Washington astride his great horse drew rein. 'Halt!' he shouted. Then he gave the command to fire. The volley and a British volley rang out simultaneously, and all were swallowed in billowing smoke. When it cleared Washington ordered the advance to continue. Then as the British were seen to begin to give way he cried out exultantly: 'Bring up the reserves! The day is ours!'

The British were so greatly outnumbered that they were forced to fall back, and they set off towards the bridge in a ragged retreat. Washington, sensing a rout, first ordered the Philadelphia Light Horse in pursuit, and then, catching the inspiration of the moment, clapped spurs to his horse and with a wild whoop gave chase himself. But he need not have bothered. The cavalry quickly scattered the redcoats and by the time he appeared on the scene the last of them were disappearing into the wood beside the post road beyond the bridge.

Washington next rode back to Princeton to see how Sullivan had been progressing. He found that the British had held out briefly in the college grounds. Nearly half of them had shut themselves in the Nassau Hall where they were surrounded. At first they had refused to give in, but when an American cannon ball had broken through the wall of their sanctuary a hundred or so of them surrendered and the rest fled eastward towards Brunswick. Washington ordered his ill-clad troops to collect what they wanted from the British stores, and most were able to equip themselves from head to toe. Soon afterwards it was learnt that Cornwallis was approaching, and Washington immediately assembled all his regiments and marched them away. They got clear long before Cornwallis's arrival, and directly it was certain they were safe from pursuit, they settled down to travel by easy stages the seventy-mile journey north to Morristown, which was to become the military capital for the rest of the winter. Thus ended a brilliant campaign and one highly significant in American history, for the spirits of all were raised by these successes, and the war was able to be continued just when all had seemed lost.

Chapter Six

PHILADELPHIA

'The best way of ending the war on terms of accommodation as moderate as their powers will admit is to invade by way of Chesapeake Bay and cause the province of Maryland to submit, which with its large proportion of loyalists would be an easy task.'

Lee's Plan of 29 March 1777.

[1]

At the time of the successful conclusion of the Trenton operation the American forces were widely scattered. There were 3,500 men at Peekskill guarding the Hudson Highlands, a slightly larger force at Ticonderoga was watching the approaches from Canada, and there were 7,000 at Morristown where Washington had his headquarters. The current military capital of Morristown, which was twenty miles west of New York and protected by a barrier of hills, was conveniently placed. Roads led to the Delaware in the west and to the Hudson in the east. A courier could arrive with dispatches from Congress in Philadelphia by noon on the day they were sent. Through Peekskill on the Hudson the way was open by river to the base at Albany and by road to New England. Morristown also could only be approached by defiles through hills and even if these were only manned by militia its capture would be costly.

The stay of the force at Morristown was not entirely trouble-free. In January an outbreak of smallpox occurred in camp and village. An attempt was made to contain the epidemic by isolation, but when this did not bring results, inoculation was resorted to, even at the risk of an enemy attack with half the men incapacitated. The order was given. The surgeons got to work. The Presbyterian and Baptist churches were used as infirmaries and filled and emptied several times in succession, and the streets were soon thronged with lively convalescents. Fortunately the enemy remained quiescent. Meanwhile, Washington himself went down

96

Martha Washington as a young woman, engraving after Alonzo Chappel

with an attack of quinsy. The doctors resorted to cupping and for a few days his staff were anxious; but he had a strong constitution conditioned by his early campaigns on the Virginia frontier and he was soon restored to good health.

Washington's recovery was assisted by the arrival at Morristown of his wife Martha. 'Lady' Washington as her contemporaries called her—since some sort of title seemed required by her husband's exalted position—was in fact quite a simple and unpretentious person. She became very popular with the ladies of the garrison, among whom were the three beautiful daughters of Governor Livingston of New Jersey who lived nearby with their aunt Lady Stirling, and before long had them organised into a sewing club for the benefit of the soldiers.

By the spring of 1777 Washington's armies were beginning to grow in numbers. The New Jersey Militia were turning out in force, the Rhode Island regiments were coming up from Peekskill, and down on the Delaware, with Benedict Arnold in command, the Pennsylvania militia were rallying to defend the river crossings. But the American

General John Burgoyne

troops were still very short of clothing and equipment, and their discipline, never of a high order, had deteriorated. A major discontent was the lack of regular pay. Besides causing men to desert this made replacements harder to get, for the officers sent on recruiting missions often lacked funds to pay the necessary bounties. In spite of his problems, however, Washington decided to take the offensive, and in May, having sent Martha back to Mount Vernon, he marched the men at Morristown away from their winter quarters to take up a position nearer the enemy.

*

The British plans for the forthcoming campaigning season were slow to materialise. The Secretary for the Colonies Lord George Germain conceived a scheme for an advance from Canada combined with one down the Mohawk and another up the Hudson. This was well received in political circles in England where the difficulties of the northern route and the danger of a flank attack from New England were ignored, but it was less popular with Howe who understood its disadvantages, and in any case preferred a westward thrust against Philadelphia. But if Howe did not approve, his junior Burgoyne certainly did. He had long been eager to lead such an expedition and directly he heard it was contemplated hurried home to try and persuade the authorities to place him in command. All through the winter he was begging interviews with a reluctant sovereign and ministers, and haranguing and lecturing anyone who would listen. Not without success, for at a Cabinet meeting held in March he was formally selected to lead the northern army. His choice instead of Carleton the commander-in-chief in Canada had a special attraction for Germain because Carleton was a political rival. George III was by no means happy to see Carleton superseded, for he believed the Governor had saved Canada; but he did not feel justified in overriding his ministers when they urged him to appoint Burgoyne. It was of course a cruel blow to Carleton. As soon as Burgoyne crossed the frontier he would be to all intents and purposes an independent general, making requisitions which would have to be supplied from the material sources of Canada but corresponding directly with the Secretary for the Colonies in London who was the Governor's notorious enemy. The situation was intolerable and Carleton sent in his resignation, but Lord North refused to accept it on the grounds that his abandonment of such a post at so critical a moment would harm British interests. George III agreed with his prime minister, saying in a letter on 2 July 1777: 'Anyone that will for an instant suppose himself in the situation of Sir Guy Carleton must feel that the resignation of the government of Quebec is the only dignified part. Though I think as things were situated, the ordering of him to remain in the province was a necessary measure, yet it must be owned to be mortifying to a soldier.'

It seemed as if Germain's plan was about to be implemented. Certainly Burgoyne's advance from Canada and St. Leger's thrust down the Mohawk from the west were put in train. Howe's contribution, however, was never satisfactorily arranged. He was not anxious to detach a large number of his troops to assist Burgoyne who he believed would manage very well on his own. He much preferred to make his major effort in the form of an attack on the American capital at Philadelphia; and he was strengthened in this when his prisoner Charles Lee unexpectedly submitted a plan for ending the war 'to both sides' advantage', which envisaged a somewhat similar operation to the one Howe had been contemplating.

Lee's plan was based on his knowledge of the conditions in Maryland and Virginia gained while in command of the Southern Department at the time of Clinton's abortive attempt to capture Charleston. He submitted it to Howe in six pages of closely written foolscap. The gist was

George III by Thomas Gainsborough

that the best way of ending the war on terms of accommodation 'as moderate as their powers will admit' was to invade by way of Chesapeake Bay and cause the province of Maryland to submit, which with its large proportion of loyalists would be an easy task. If at the same time the people of Virginia were prevented from sending aid and the Pennsylvanians held off, 'the whole is dissolved, a period put to the war . . . and all the inhabitants of that great tract southward of the Patapsico and lying between the Potomac and Chesapeake Bay and those on the shore of Maryland will immediately lay down their arms'.

Howe had originally agreed to send a force up the Hudson to coordinate with Burgoyne's expedition from Canada. Later, however, he dispatched to London the draft of his new plan under which the bulk of his effort was directed against Philadelphia. Although the alteration was conscientiously submitted to Germain it took so long to cross the Atlantic and reach him that the Secretary for the Colonies could have done little about it even if he had wanted to. In the event, he unwisely set in motion the expeditions from north and west without making certain that Howe would cooperate by sending up the Hudson a sizeable force.

The Americans were at first handicapped by a clash of personalities. The commander of the Northern Department was the New Yorker Philip John Schuyler who had the misfortune to be heartily disliked by New Englanders. It stemmed from an old argument over the respective rights of New York and Massachusetts Bay to the territory which is now Vermont and was then known as the Hampshire Grants. On more than one occasion high-handed action was taken by the authorities of New York, and Schuyler as a leading citizen and large landowner in that colony became identified with proceedings which the whole of New England considered unjust. Consequently the New England militia came to Schuyler's assistance reluctantly, and when they arrived made every effort to leave again on the flimsiest of pretexts. The New England delegates to Congress, including John and Samuel Adams, were also mainly Schuyler's ill-wishers and sought to replace him.

At this time, Crown Point had been recovered by the British and Ticonderoga was the frontier fortress of the rebellion. The garrison was commanded by Major General Horatio Gates, a soldier of the lobby rather than of the skirmish line. During the siege of Boston, Gates had been adjutant general in the camp at Cambridge. While there he was at great pains to ingratiate himself with the New Englanders; and he managed to establish an intimate and profitable alliance with the region's

*Major General Horatio Gates by
Alonzo Chappel*

politicians. As soon as Gates was installed at Ticonderoga he set himself
down to the business of undermining, overthrowing and supplanting his
superior officer. For three months he despatched by every post letters to
the New England members of Congress filled with charges and innuen-
does against his chief, along with artful illusions to the popularity of himself among the New Englanders. Then, he applied for leave of absence on
the plea of poor health, and followed his correspondence in person to
where Congress was sitting.[1] He worked very hard urging his claims, and
at last received the reward of his importunity, for he was ordered by a resolution of Congress to go immediately to Ticonderoga and there assume
command of the field army.

Schuyler, deeply hurt, now sprang into action. Having persuaded a
New York convention to elect him as a delegate to Congress, he went to
Philadelphia and demanded an official enquiry into his past conduct; and
Congress were so impressed by the result of the inquiry and by his digni-
fied bearing that he was again invested with absolute military control of

[1] First Baltimore and then Philadelphia.

the Northern Department. On hearing this, Gates, who had proceeded no further than Albany, posted back to Congress boiling with indignation and intent on demanding his rights.

All this happened at an unfortunate moment, for Schuyler had hardly resumed his functions at Albany before he heard that Burgoyne's army was concentrating on the frontier and that Seneca warriors and loyalists were mustering at the head of the Mohawk River. In the absence of Gates, the defence of the important fortress of Ticonderoga was committed to Major General St. Clair; but the task proved too much for him. His weak brigade was driven out, and its battered remnants joined Schuyler at Fort Edward on 12 July 1777. A few days later the combined force had to fall back again, Schuyler doing his best to delay the enemy advance by laying waste the countryside over which the British would travel. Axemen felled forest trees in interlacing heaps across the roads; bridges were destroyed over creeks and rivers; swamps were created by rough dams; and most of the settlers, obeying Schuyler's call, fell back after burning their standing crops and scattering their cattle. But it was in vain. The British pressed on. All this aggravated the resentment against Schuyler and to

General Philip Schuyler by Alonzo Chappel

counteract sectional antagonism Washington hurried north both Benedict Arnold and Benjamin Lincoln to assist the commander in the Northern Department. In the absence of Gates, Arnold became Schuyler's second-in-command, and Lincoln took charge of the New

England militia. It was not enough. The American cause had been shaken by the fall of Ticonderoga. With rumours of treason rumbling in its ears, Congress reacted. St. Clair was relieved; Schuyler bowed out; and on 4 August Gates was appointed, for the second time, to take over the Northern Department. He was thus in command when one of the decisive battles of the war was fought at Saratoga, and this had far-reaching results for Washington personally.

*

In response to Washington's move south from Morristown, Howe first sent reinforcements to Brunswick to bring up the numbers of the garrison to 18,000 and then on 14 June despatched a force towards Somerset Court House to try and cut off the American detachment at Princeton and entice Washington into a battle in the open. Washington, however, who had occupied a strong position at Middlebrook ten miles from Brunswick, was not to be tempted away from his stronghold. During the following days Howe continued manoeuvring; but the Americans managed to avoid a major engagement, and finally, on 28 June, the British began to retire first to Amboy and then on over the water to Staten Island, the result being that by the end of the month most of them had left New Jersey.

Although Washington soon learnt that the British had gone, he was nevertheless still in doubt as to their next move, although an early indication that preparations were in progress for a substantial expedition came when spies reported that transports were being fitted with horse-boxes, and stored with water, forage and provisions for a month's voyage. The destination of the British force might equally well be Boston to the east, Philadelphia to the south-west or Albany to the north; but, believing the last to be the most likely, Washington marched his army towards West Point.

On 24 July Washington heard that Howe had set sail on the previous day not up the Hudson but out to sea from Sandy Hook. On the last day of the month more news came, this time from watchers along the coast reporting that some two hundred sail appeared to be entering the estuary of the Delaware as if to go up-river and assault Philadelphia. Realising that Congress would expect him to try and defend the capital, Washington immediately rode off towards Philadelphia. On the way he was told that the British vessels had now put out to sea again, and, wondering whether the whole manoeuvre might not be just a hoax to lure him away from the Hudson area, he decided to wait on further events and quartered his troops twenty miles short of Philadelphia.

It was a fortnight before Washington heard anything more. Then news came that the royal fleet had appeared at the entrance of Chesapeake Bay. On this he immediately marched his men towards the capital he had to defend and which now appeared about to be attacked from the west. After a short halt on the outskirts Washington led his troops in a show of force through the main streets. Astride his massive charger, the leader was more impressive than the followers who lacked uniformity except for a green sprig in their hats, and whose clothing was ragged and marching far from precise; but they stepped out proudly to the sound of fife and drum and spectators cheered them lustily all along the route.

Shortly before Washington reached Philadelphia, the Marquis de Lafayette had arrived to report to Congress. An avid republican, he came to America to offer his services and his fortune to the cause of freedom. He had met, however, with a chilling initial reception. Congress made him wait in the street while a delegate was fetched who spoke his language, and he was then told in fairly intelligible French that he was a troublesome adventurer and that Philadelphia contained too many of his sort already.

Lafayette was not willing to be dismissed in this unceremonious fashion. He insisted on being seen personally by Congress, and when finally they agreed to interview him, he put his case in a most appealing way by presenting a list of the sacrifices he was proposing to make for the American cause, and claiming nothing, except the right to serve at his own expense. Congress who had already been impressed by his proud bearing and quiet tone soon came to realise that here was a most uncommon specimen of a foreign mercenary; so without further ado they nominated him an unattached major general, an appointment later approved by Washington. In the forthcoming engagement, however, Lafayette was to act only in a minor capacity as a member of Washington's staff.

On leaving Philadelphia Washington felt the need of Morgan's riflemen who had been sent to assist Gates, and to take their place he organised a picked force from his brigades. When these had been assembled he sent them forward under William Maxwell to delay Howe's advance. Next, having drawn up the main body at Wilmington, he rode forward to Elk Town and set about stripping the countryside by sending away stores from the magazines and seeing that granaries were emptied and horses and carts removed all along the line the British were likely to follow towards Philadelphia.

General Lafayette by Charles Willson Peale

*

Although Howe might very well have reached a spot to disembark unopposed nearer the capital by continuing up the Delaware, his plan of going round by Chesapeake Bay and the Head of Elk succeeded in puzzling Washington, though at the expense of additional discomfort for his troops. These had endured enough foul weather to make most of them sea-sick, but generally the wind was dead and the heat more troublesome. If conditions were bad in the open sea, they were even worse in the close waters of Chesapeake Bay. According to the journal of John Montrésor, Howe's chief engineer, the cabins became as stifling and foetid as the hold of a slaver. Still, however circuitous the journey and however many weeks spent at sea, the British eventually reached their intended landing place. On 25 August they began to disembark near the Head of Elk in north-east Maryland. It was no easy matter, for the Elk river was full of shoals and sandbanks. Admiral Lord Howe was nevertheless not daunted. He stationed boats to mark the points of danger; he sent the larger vessels to plough channels through the muddy bars; and he took as his flagship the man-of-war that made its way farthest to the front. Thanks to his efforts, before dark on the 26th every soldier, field-piece and wagon was ashore.

There were, however, disappointments for the British following their successful landing. General Howe had been told by Lee to expect help from the local population, but because of Washington's efforts at laying waste the countryside, this was not forthcoming. As Captain Richard Fitzpatrick of Howe's army was to write: 'The inhabitants are almost all fled from their houses, and have driven their cattle with them so we do not live very luxuriously though in a country that has every appearance of plenty.'

The first encounter took place at Cooch's Bridge, six miles from the Head of Elk, where Maxwell's men and the local militia opened fire and attempted to halt the British advance. The Americans, however, were not in sufficient numbers to do very much and were withdrawn after the enemy had deployed. Meanwhile Washington, having decided that the position at Wilmington was too exposed, had led his men back twenty miles along the road to Philadelphia and placed them in a defensive position behind Brandywine Creek whose steep sides formed a considerable obstacle. Here he covered the main road which after passing through the small town of Kennett Square turned east and crossed the creek at Chadd's Ford. Washington left Bland's cavalry and Maxwell's marksmen to delay the enemy on the west of the stream and then placed Greene's division in a position to guard Chadd's crossing with Wayne to the north and Sullivan still farther upstream. He placed Hazen's Canadians four miles to the north and he put Armstrong's militia along cliffs south of the crossing.

Howe's plan to force the passage of the Brandywine resembled closely the one he had used so successfully on Long Island the year before. After concentrating in Kennett Square four miles west of the American position he divided his force into two columns. The task of the first, which included the Hessians and was under Knyphausen, was to advance straight down the main road and make a feint frontal attack. Meanwhile, the second column under Cornwallis was to march off along the valley road in the direction of the fords over the creek and its tributaries some five miles to the north and make a flank attack.

The Hessians brushed with Maxwell's men and drove them over the creek, then they made ostentatious arrangements for an assault on the centre of the American position. This, as it was meant to do, so occupied the minds of Washington and his staff that they paid little attention to the enemy column plodding north along the valley road.

The first intimation of a flank attack was a message from Hazen's Canadians saying an enemy column was on the march on the other side of the stream, whereupon Washington ordered the cavalry to investigate, and in due course heard from Bland, and also from a scouting party of the 8th Pennsylvania Regiment, that British troops were indeed moving north.

Washington then very nearly made a false move. Considering that the enemy opposite must have been weakened to provide the force marching away, he planned a frontal attack of his own. The order for this had barely been drawn up, however, before a conflicting message arrived from Sullivan announcing that a thorough reconnaissance had been made across the stream and that no British troops had been discovered in the vicinity of the upper fords. Washington now did not know what to believe, and he paused for a period to await further news. The matter was finally resolved when a local resident named Thomas Cheney galloped up and sought an interview. After the staff had reluctantly brought him before the general, Cheney announced breathlessly that the British were across the Brandywine and at that very moment were approaching the Birmingham meeting house only a mile or so away. It seemed impossible. How could they have reached that far? Particularly in the light of Sullivan's message. But Cheney was so vehement that Washington called off the frontal attack and without further ado set about making the necessary moves to protect his threatened flank. He placed Sullivan who was already in the area in command, and he ordered the reserve divisions of Stirling and Stephen to march immediately to reinforce him.

The new dispositions were completed with commendable promptness once the orders were given, but they were nevertheless made too late to be effective, for Cornwallis's men were approaching long before a defence line had been properly established. Sullivan's men who were already in position stood firm at first, but when a most forceful attack developed they started to give way, and it was not long before they were falling back in disorder. The reserves arrived in time to avert a complete rout, but when darkness fell only a withdrawal from the field of battle could save the Americans from disaster. While the British were attacking in the north, the Hessians were storming across the creek. Covered by cannon fire they at first drove back the Americans in confusion. Wayne's men then managed to bring their own cannon into action, and their final withdrawal was made in an orderly fashion. In the course of the night most of the Americans managed to march the twelve miles to Chester where, having been put into some sort of order by Washington and his officers, they bivouacked until dawn.

The records of American losses in the battles are even more unreliable than usual, but it would seem they suffered at least 1,000 casualties, 400 men also being taken prisoner—at least twice the British loss. Nevertheless, they did not appear greatly depressed. They wrongly believed they had suffered fewer casualties than their opponents; they considered they had not done too badly against the professionals; and they marched off back to Philadelphia in a remarkably cheerful state of mind for a defeated army.

[2]

On reaching Philadelphia, Washington found that Congress had departed hastily for Lancaster. He also learnt that the ruling body had handed over to him supreme control, and he decided not to remain and defend the capital. Instead, having replenished his stores from the magazines, he recrossed the Schuylkill and attempted to block the British approach. It seemed as if the two sides were going to meet head on, but a sudden downpour dampened the powder, and Washington felt compelled to disengage and march north to Warwick to get a fresh supply of this essential article.

The new American move gave the British the opportunity of entering Philadelphia, for only Wayne's brigade was left in the woods near Paoli to dispute their passage. It was Wayne's home country and he assured Washington that he would be able to hide from the British and attack them in the rear directly they attempted to cross the Schuylkill. It did not, however, work out like this. The people of the district were Tories, and Howe learnt from them of Wayne's position and intentions and sent in Major General Charles Grey in a surprise attack.

Grey selected five battalions for the task and ordered them to use only their bayonets. To make surprise certain he gave instructions that the flints were to be removed from every musket—thereby becoming known afterwards as 'No Flint' Grey. If Wayne had not posted guards and seen they kept alert, his entire command might well have been wiped out. As it was, the hastily aroused Americans resisted manfully and Wayne was able to withdraw at least some of them along with four cannon, although 150 Americans were killed, wounded or captured whereas Grey only suffered seven casualties. Word of this grim demonstration of British skill with the bayonet spread rapidly throughout Washington's army, and many militiamen soon found pressing business to draw them home. Trevelyan, writing about the incident, said: 'The affair has often been called unfairly and absurdly the massacre of Paoli. Men always attach the idea of cruelty to modes of warfare in which they themselves are not proficient; and Americans liked the bayonet as little as Englishmen approved of taking deliberate aim at individual officers. It was currently reported throughout the Confederacy that quarter had been refused and that the wounded were stabbed where they lay; but there is no arguing against figures. When the neighbouring farmers assembled next morning to bury their fallen countrymen, they found only fifty-three dead bodies.'

*

On 21 September 1777 Howe moved north-west, and Washington unwittingly marched to meet him. It was a ruse to draw the Americans away from the Schuylkill fords and having neatly done so Howe turned, passed through Valley Forge, and with what may have been an uncanny prescience not only destroyed the forge but rounded up all the stock to be found on the neighbouring farms. The British continued down the west bank of the Schuylkill and crossed at Swede's Ford. Then, turning south, they occupied the small town of Germantown five miles north of the capital and began making plans for the investment of Philadelphia. A formal siege, however, was not found necessary, for the advanced troops under Cornwallis met with no opposition as they approached, and were able to move straight in. As the redcoats marched through the streets with bands playing, they were cheered by thousands of spectators, mostly women and children. Some of the latter many years afterwards were to speak of their youthful impressions of the scene. One man who was only ten at the time was greatly impressed. 'I went up to the grenadiers in the leading column when they entered Second Street,' he said, 'and several spoke to me in a most kindly way. The looks of the Hessians who followed the grenadiers were terrific. Their brass caps, their moustachios, their countenances by nature morose, all impressed me, and their music sounded in better English than they themselves could speak, "Plunder! Plunder!"' Some of the older ones, indeed, could not help comparing this brilliant procession with the dilapidated army that had passed down the same line of streets a few weeks before.

*

In spite of the many setbacks he had met with, Washington was still eager to come to grips with the enemy again. He sought another opportunity like the one he had been presented with at Trenton, and early in October believed he had such a chance when he learnt from an intercepted letter that Howe had divided his army and sent a large detachment to attack American fortresses on the Delaware. Washington now decided to try and capture what he thought was the lightly defended enemy camp at Germantown. He knew the region well. His army had been in and around the place several times in the past month, and he had at one time considered defending Philadelphia in the area where Howe's men were now installed. From his spies he had received a good description of the British dispositions and with the assistance of his staff set about forthwith drawing up plans for a night march and a surprise attack.

*

Four roads led to Germantown from Washington's position by Pennypacker's Mills, and he proposed to despatch a column down each one of them, so that they might arrive together after an all-night march. The militia under Armstrong were to follow the western road beside the Schuylkill, Greene was to use the two parallel eastern roads, and Washington, aware of much criticism of Sullivan's performance at Brandywine, decided to accompany the latter's column in the centre.

In spite of careful preparations beforehand, the approach march was not carried out well. Greene's men who had the farthest to go lost their way and the result was that they arrived half an hour later than Sullivan's. It was the advanced troops of Conway's brigade in Sullivan's column who were the first to engage. They brushed with an enemy light infantry patrol and immediately formed a line of battle. There followed a brisk little engagement in which the numerically superior Americans forced back first the light infantry and then elements of the 40th Regiment led by Colonel Musgrave who had come up in support. Howe, hearing the firing, rode up to find out what was happening. He was greatly shocked to see his light infantry falling back in confusion. 'For shame, Light Infantry,' he cried out. 'Form! Form! It's only a scouting party.' Just at that moment a high enemy volley struck some branches above his head and dropped a debris of leaves on his shoulders so that, somewhat disheartened, he wasted no more time attempting to rally his outpost troops and galloped back to set up a more solid line of defence in the rear. Meanwhile, Musgrave, battling manfully to rally his retreating troops, had reached Chew House just east of the road Sullivan's column

General Nathanael Greene by
Charles Willson Peale

had been following. Although a fog was descending he managed to gather a number of his men inside the mansion and in a short space of time turned it into something like a fortress by getting his troops to bar the doors, fill the hallway with furniture and poke portholes in the shuttered windows.

Musgrave's staunch defence of Chew House robbed the Americans of victory, for Washington decided to hold up the advance until the enemy stronghold had been reduced, and this caused the whole impetus of his attack to flag. To make matters worse Stephen's men collided with Wayne's who were lost in the fog and shot them up believing they were enemy; and Greene's division, arriving late on the flank, after making some progress, was first halted when the British brought up reinforcements, and then forced back in confusion.

All this was a prelude to a general American withdrawal. The moment of victory had come. It had flickered with uncertainty for a brief space. Then it had passed. Once again Howe had won the day. Washington had marched his army twenty miles the night before to get at the British. Now he marched them all the way back again.

The Americans had suffered twice as many casualties as the British, but Howe made no attempt to follow up his victory. Instead, shortly after the battle, he evacuated Germantown and consolidated his army in Philadelphia.

A pleasing footnote to the affair is the story of the British commander's dog. Wayne it seems was not the only one to be lost in the fog at Germantown. It was so thick that even Howe's dog could not find his way around. He fell in with Washington's men and went with them all the way to Pennypacker's Mills before he discovered his mistake. After he reached the American camp and his identity[1] had been established, he was haled before the general. Washington was too fond of his own dogs to keep the pet of another, and, even with the many things of real importance that he had to do, found time to write a brief note to Howe which he sent back with the dog. This read: 'General Washington's compliments to General Howe—does himself the pleasure to return to him a dog which accidentally fell into his hands and by the inscription on the collar appears to belong to General Howe.'

*

After a short period of inactivity Howe began operations to clear the long river approach to Philadelphia. The first obstacle when approaching from the sea was the unfinished redoubt at Billingsport. Although not very strong it had guns emplaced and across the channel towards Chester stretched a double line of *chevaux de frise* which would rip the bottom out of any seagoing vessel attempting to sail upstream. Further north and just below the mouth of the Schuylkill were three more lines of *chevaux de frise* protected by the guns of the earth-walled Fort Mercer on the east bank of the Delaware and those of the more formidable Fort Mifflin on the west bank. Finally, between these two forts and Philadelphia lay a small American flotilla at anchor.

The first move was made by the Americans when some ships of their squadron sailed north and attacked the Philadelphia waterfront. It was an abortive affair, for one of the two frigates ran aground and was forced to surrender after receiving a severe hammering from British guns, and the rest were able to make little impression on the enemy.

On 2 October, as his brother's fleet was approaching the defences, Howe sent two regiments from Chester across the Delaware against Billingsport. Unfinished as it was, the garrison spiked their guns and departed so that the British were able to remove the *chevaux de frise* which

---

[1] Pontigaud 47.

the fort had guarded, and when the warships arrived they could sail up towards the next obstacle. On 22 October the Hessians were sent in against Fort Mercer. They forced their way through the protective ring of abatis, but on entering the ditch under the walls were met with such murderous short-range fire that they were driven back, suffering many casualties and having their commander Colonel von Donop mortally wounded. During this attack the British naval squadron also suffered severely. Three ships went aground on a mudbank below the fort and two of these could not be refloated. The Americans concentrated their fire on the hulks and drifted flaming rafts downstream to come to rest beside them. The result was that both were set alight and one blew up when the flames reached the magazine. Benefitting from this disastrous experience, the British next staged a better coordinated attack on neighbouring Fort Mifflin. Numerous batteries were emplaced on the west bank to pound the fort from the flank, and then the warships sailed up and opened fire, one sloop even taking a channel between the fort and the mainland and hammering the fort with her 24-pounders at a range of less than one hundred yards. For six days the garrison endured one of the most concentrated bombardments of the war, every night the wounded being evacuated and reinforcements being brought up by water to replace them. However, once all the guns were out of action, and many casualties had been suffered, the fort was evacuated. Cornwallis next crossed the river with some of his best troops and attacked Fort Mercer which a reinforced British naval squadron had brought under fire from the rear, and on 22 November this strong-point was also abandoned. Finally, what remained of the American flotilla was destroyed by Admiral Howe's more powerful squadron and the British found themselves not only in complete control of Philadelphia but also possessing a secure lifeline for supply by sea.

*

Before the arrival of the British in Philadelphia its population had been greatly reduced in numbers. Many Quaker families had earlier been forcibly evacuated to Virginia because of their non-cooperation with the patriots; officials like the delegates to Congress had departed; and many private families had left with their portable possessions fearing these might otherwise fall into the hands of the Hessians. The result was that there was ample room for the newcomers. There was plenty of food too, for in spite of Washington's patrols the farmers and countrywomen continued to bring in stock and provisions to sell, being attracted by the hard money paid, which was so much more valuable than the patriots' paper currency. Also, with the opening up of the river, provisions which included wine and grog started to enter the capital by sea, and a horde of sutlers and hucksters, Tories all and Scotsmen nearly to a man, arrived and distributed among themselves the most desirable places of business left vacant by the hurried departure of the Whig traders and filled the shopfronts with goods. Thus the officers and their friends were to have a gay and comfortable winter and the ladies of Philadelphia the chance of joining in the garrison's gaieties. The only slight social problem was in the person of the too amiable lady that Sir William Howe brought with him. Just when he fell in with the notorious Mrs. Loring is not recorded but he seems to have met her soon after coming to America. Little is known of the lady herself save that she was a Miss Lloyd and had been married to Joseph Loring when he was a High Sheriff. After Mrs. Loring became his mistress Howe appointed the compliant Loring commissioner of prisons, a post from which a handsome graft could be taken, and from then on Loring and Mrs. Loring always accompanied the general. Thus the sedate and strait-laced females of Philadelphia were faced with the choice of either forgoing a gay season or accepting the commander-in-chief's discreditable companion as their social leader. Perhaps understandably it did not take long for most of them to decide that they would ignore their distaste for the lady and take part in the most brilliant season their town had ever known.

There was little military activity that winter except for a few skirmishes that took place when rival foraging parties brushed with one another. These together with an odd little river encounter provided the sum total of the exchanges. The last stemmed from an invention of David Bushnell of Connecticut who had earlier created the *Turtle*, a barrel-like craft capable of submersion and operated by turning paddles with a crank. It had been used in August 1776 against a British ship lying at anchor in New York Bay. The sole operator tried to bore a hole in the ship's bottom but was defeated by the thickness of the copper sheathing, and then paddled away pursued by a British barge. Fearing capture with the explosive in his possession he released it and made off. A few minutes later it exploded harmlessly. Then, before another attempt could be made, New York was evacuated and the vessel destroyed in case it should fall into enemy hands. Bushnell did not attempt to build another submarine, but in 1777 he designed a crude contact mine by attaching a gunlock as a fuse to a floating keg of gunpowder. These devices proved to be of more practical use than the submarine, for one of them sank a British schooner in the Connecticut River. Following on this success Bushnell was instructed to loose some of his mines against British shipping in the Delaware River at Philadelphia.

Bushnell decided to conduct the operation on a large scale and, before starting, assembled a hundred of his contraptions. He managed to send the kegs off down-river without much difficulty, but as the channel was almost choked with floating ice not one of them came into contact with a British vessel. However, the attempt caused considerable alarm among the British garrison and in an extended display of nerves soldiers and sailors continued to fire at any flotsam on the river for several days. The reaction of the Americans to their opponents' antics was one of ribald amusement, as is clearly shown in the written accounts of the incident at the time. For example, the *New Jersey Gazette* reported the affair as follows:

> The battle began, and it was surprising to behold the incessant blaze that was kept up against the enemy, the kegs. Both Officers and Men exhibited the most unparallel skill and bravery on the occasion; while the citizens stood gazing in solemn witness of their prowess. From the *Roebuck* and other ships of war whole broadsides were poured into the Delaware. In short, not a wandering ship, stick or drift log, but felt the vigor of British arms. The action began about sunrise, and would have been completed with great success by noon had not an old market woman coming down the river with provisions, unfortunately let a small keg of butter fall overboard, which (as it was the ebb) floated down to the seat of action. At the sight of this unexpected reinforcement of the enemy, the battle was renewed with fresh fury, and the firing was incessant until evening closed the affair. The kegs were either totally demolished or obliged to fly, as none of them have shown their heads since. It is said his Excellency Lord Howe has dispatched a swift sailing packet with an account of this victory to the Court in London. On a word, Monday the Fifth of January 1778 must ever be distinguished for the memorable Battle of the Kegs.

Another example was a ballad by the New Jersey Congressman Francis Hopkinson. Written in the same vein as the *Gazette*'s report, it became very popular even in Philadelphia itself, for although Howe was much loved by his men they nevertheless took a great delight in having a good laugh at his expense. The quatrain of the ballad that pleased the British servicemen most ran:

> Sir William, he, as snug as a flea
> Lay all this time a-snoring;
> Nor dreamed of harm, as he lay warm
> In bed with Mrs. Loring.

Sir William had not been greatly concerned about the downrush of the kegs, and in any case was not one to mind a joke against himself. His period of command was nearly over. In October he had submitted to Lord Germain his application to be relieved. A few months later he learnt that his request had been approved. Now he was waiting for the arrival of his successor before sailing to England and he saw no reason to suffer undue boredom.

Chapter Seven

VALLEY FORGE

'In December 1777 Washington determined to remain at a point where
he could hold the Royal foraging parties in respect throughout the
winter, and be near at hand, when spring came, to avail himself of the
very earliest opportunity for turning the tables upon his adversary. He
stationed his army . . . at Valley Forge . . . a name which bids fair to be
the most celebrated encampment in the world's history.'

Trevelyan

After the fall of the forts guarding the estuary of the River Delaware, the
Americans went into camp at Whitemarsh, twelve miles north of Phila-
delphia. During this period the war took a new turn. On 6 October a
British force stormed the forts[1] of Montgomery and Clinton guarding the
Hudson and it seemed as if a way was being opened for an attack on the
American base at Albany, and perhaps a link up from the south with
Burgoyne's force advancing from Canada. But soon after the receipt of
this news came the announcement that the British coming from Canada
had been defeated first at Freeman's Farm, then on the Bemis Heights, and
had finally surrendered at Saratoga. Earlier, Generals Schuyler and St.
Clair had been in command in the north; but the fall of Fort Ticonderoga
on Lake George and a successful British raid on the base at Bennington
had led to Schuyler resigning and St. Clair being replaced. Their suc-
cessors were Major General Horatio Gates and Benedict Arnold. In view
of his praiseworthy vigour and leadership during a British raid on the
American base at Danbury, Connecticut, Arnold had been made a major
general. He was to prove valuable indeed in the northern campaign. First,
he took a detachment up the River Mohawk and turned back an expedition comprised of Canadians and Indians under St. Leger. Then, he
returned and played the major role in the battles fought against
Burgoyne's troops on the west bank of the Hudson some twenty miles

[1] Replaced by a defence post built at West Point farther north with a chain barrier
across the river.

from Albany. Gates as supreme commander received the honours, but it was Benedict Arnold who was the true architect of this decisive American victory.

The Americans in Pennsylvania had fought well at Brandywine Creek and Germanton, and had not been unduly downcast at their failures, but the news of the success at Saratoga not unnaturally raised their spirits and caused them to look forward to another engagement in which they could show they were as good fighters as their comrades in the north. Washington too, at first, was gratified personally as well as officially, because he felt he had done all in his power by sending reinforcements first to Schuyler and St. Clair and then to Gates. But he and many other persons were soon to be much irritated by repercussions from the success in the north.

The trouble began when Gates sent the official dispatches announcing his victory direct to Congress instead of through the commander-in-chief. Gates employed young Colonel James Wilkinson to take the dispatches, and Wilkinson not only took a very long while to travel to York, Pennsylvania where Congress was sitting, but was indiscreet enough to disclose disparaging remarks about Washington in a letter from General Conway to General Gates to one of Lord Stirling's aides when he visited that general's headquarters on the way. Gates had also requested that Wilkinson be rewarded for taking the news of the victory by promotion to brigadier general. When Congress complied, practically every colonel in the army threatened to resign.

The relevant passage in Conway's letter read: 'Heaven had determined to save your Country; or a weak General and bad Councellors would have ruined it.' Lord Stirling, in a letter to Washington about rope ferries over the Schuylkill and other minor military matters, included Conway's derogatory comment as an enclosure, explaining that it had been communicated by Wilkinson to one of his aides and he thought Washington should know about 'such wicked duplicity of conduct'.

Conway had been a problem from the start. Having served for thirty years in the French army he considered he should be made a major general, but there were twenty-three Americans all senior to him in date of rank, and these were incensed that Congress should even consider promoting him over their heads. There is no doubt that Conway was slandering Washington as a way of suggesting his own superior military genius. In fact he appeared to be willing to further his own cause by any means. Still he had shown prowess at Brandywine and Germantown, for he managed to create in Sullivan's mind a respect that amounted almost to awe, so that the general wrote that 'the regulations in his Brigade are much better than any in the army, and his knowledge of military matters in general far exceeds any officer we have'.[1] This was also Conway's own opinion, freely admitted to other officers and, as occasion offered, to Congress. For example, two weeks after Brandywine he addressed to John Hancock at York a letter[2] that began: 'It is with infinite concern that I find myself slighted and forgot when you have offered rank to officers who cost you a great deal of money and have never rendered you the least service. Baron de Kalb to whom you have offered the rank of Major General after having given him vast sums of money is my inferior in France.'

Conway also visited widely and discussed personalities without restraint. On one occasion he is said to have remarked: 'No man was more a gentleman than George Washington, or appeared to more advantage at his table, or in the usual intercourse of life; but as to his talents for the command of an Army, they were miserable indeed.'

Another way in which Conway tried to advance his claim for promotion was by trying to get Washington replaced by Gates, because the latter was more favourably disposed towards him. In this he had the support of Thomas Mifflin the quartermaster general who had become alienated from Washington in the summer of 1777 when the commander-in-chief would not follow his advice and take immediate steps to defend Philadelphia. A number of members of Congress had also lost faith in the commander-in-chief. John Adams of Massachusetts thought that Washington had too much power, was being treated like a demi-god by his officers, and that it would be wise to appoint someone else. Dr. Benjamin Rush, formerly senior medical superintendent, was found to be the writer of a missive that came into the hands of Patrick Henry which read: 'The northern army has shown us what Americans are capable of doing with a General at their head. The spirit of the southern army is in no way inferior to the spirit of the northern. A Gates, a Lee or a Conway would in a few weeks render them an irrestible body of men.' James Duane of New York was also found to be active in denigrating Washington; and James Lovell of Massachusetts, a schoolmaster and a man of the greatest assiduity in his work, possessed a high regard for Gates, like many of the leaders in New England, and carried on with him a correspondence that contained numerous slurs on the commander-in-chief.

[1] Sullivan Papers, 577.
[2] 159 Papers Cont. Cong. 543, L.C.

Washington, when the matter came into the open, dealt with it in his own inimitable way. First he wrote to Conway and quoted the derogatory remark made in the letter to Gates; and then he suggested to Congress, after explaining all about the matter, that he was more than ready to hand over command if they considered he was not doing his job satisfactorily—and if a worthy successor could be found. He indicated that he did not personally consider that Gates was such a person; and this was soon to become strikingly obvious when troops returning from the northern campaign revealed that the victory at Saratoga had been almost entirely due to the efforts of Benedict Arnold, and that Gates had not left his headquarters or made any attempt to lead in the field.

On being accused, Conway at first denied having written in the vein suggested; but weakened his refutation by claiming that it was the custom in Europe for junior commanders to criticise commanders-in-chief. Gates for his part complained sourly that Washington's associates must have been tampering with his mail. Both generals appeared distressed that their intrigues had been revealed, and they soon began to produce involved, verbose statements which seemed something like apologies. After this the troubles that followed from Gates's victory at Saratoga and from the machinations of the Conway cabal began to fade into oblivion. In fact, Congress was soon able to assure Washington that they had every confidence in him—though with slight reservations. Their views on the matter are indicated in a letter written by the new President Henry Laurens[1] to General Lafayette on 12 January 1778: 'I think the friends of our brave and virtuous General may rest assured that he is out of reach of his enemies, if he has an enemy, a fact of which I am in doubt of . . . All men acknowledge General Washington's virtue, his personal bravery; nor do I ever hear his military abilities questioned but comparatively with the fortunate event [Burgoyne's defeat] you allude to.'[2]

*

At a council of war held at Whitemarsh early in November, General Wayne pressed Washington to stage an attack on Philadelphia; but the American army then consisted of only 8,000 Continentals and 2,700 militia, and of the latter nearly 2,000 from Virginia and Maryland would soon be going home, while Howe had not less than 10,000 well-trained men available for the defence of the city. Bearing this in mind, eleven of the generals voted against attacking. Among these were Sullivan, Knox, and

[1] Laurens's son was one of Washington's most loyal and active aides.
[2] 3 Burnett 29.

de Kalb who had been given a division the day before; and their opinion was supported by Duportail, late captain of engineers in the French service, who had made a thorough study of the fortifications that Howe had been building. He considered that the army had neither the numbers required nor sufficient siege guns to carry out a proper siege.

The British position in fact was a strong one. A line of fortifications had been built in the north stretching from the Schuylkill to the Delaware. This included a number of redoubts in which cannon were emplaced, and the intervals were closed with abatis. With rivers guarding all the other sides, Howe and his men were well protected.

At the beginning of December, directly the supply line up the Delaware had been assured, the British staged an attack on the American lines about Whitemarsh. This was intended as a surprise, but they were not all Tories in Philadelphia, and Mrs. Lydia Darrah in whose house Captain André lodged listened in to a conference held in the dining-room and contrived to inform Washington of the British plans. The result was that the British could make no inroad on the well-prepared American line and eventually withdrew having achieved nothing.

Not long after this raid it was decided to move the American army farther away from the city. Because of the predominantly Tory sympathies of the local people information was hard to come by; and no sooner had the Americans crossed to the west bank of the Schuylkill than they ran into a 4,000-strong foraging party under Cornwallis which drove them back to the east side again. However, on the following morning, after Cornwallis had completed his mission and returned to Philadelphia, they were able to cross a little higher up-river without hindrance. Some of them used a bridge of rafts; the rest, a series of wagons lined up to form a foot-bridge so shakily connected with fence rails that the men had to go over in single file. They bivouacked that night at Gulph Mills, a dreary place on which Surgeon Albigense Waldo commented aptly: 'Not an improper name.' They were without tents, blankets and even rum, and it was snowing hard. For a week they lay at Gulph, short of food, and with but a single day of fine weather. Yet spirits remained high even before the baggage train came up and tents were pitched for the first time. Finally they marched on the few more miles to their goal. This was a wooded plateau near Valley Forge. Lying between Valley and Turtle creeks and with the river Schuylkill at its back, this natural stronghold was to become their fortified encampment for the rest of the winter.

*

Valley Forge was a small village on the west bank of the Schuylkill, some twenty-two miles from Philadelphia. At one time it possessed saw and grist mills and, as its name implies, a forge used to manufacture munitions for the American army. The forge was built on a plot of 175 acres which was part of a land grant made by William Penn to his daughter Letitia in 1701. It passed into the hands of the Potts family, and one Isaac Potts was the owner during the Revolution. As already related, in late September 1777 the British raided the village, destroyed the forge, and drove off the livestock of the neighbouring farms.

The decision by the council of war to set up winter quarters at Valley Forge was not unanimous; but bearing in mind that Pennsylvania and New Jersey were demanding protection from British raids and that it was not possible to billet the soldiers in the nearby towns because they were already swollen with refugees, Valley Forge was as good a place as any. It was near enough to the enemy to give protection to the neighbourhood and could be made strong by entrenching. Howe later testified to its strength by saying that when he heard it was being fortified he dropped all thought of attacking.

According to Surgeon Albigense Waldo, Washington told his generals to consult the chief engineer Duportail 'on the proper and necessary means to execute the works', and the redoubts and entrenchments were constructed in accordance with plans drawn up by the Frenchman. The inner line consisted of parallel entrenchments, having a wall and ditch on one side and abatis on the other, and these linked two strong points named Star Redoubt and Fort Huntington near the Schuylkill with another called Fort Washington by Valley Creek. The outer line nearer the enemy started with the strong points called Fort Greene and Fort Muhlenberg and stretched westward along the southern edge of the plateau to join the inner line at Fort Washington. When the defences were completed all the approaches to the camp were covered. Star Redoubt commanded the Schuylkill, Fort Huntington covered the western approaches, Fort Washington overlooked the Chester County valley, and Fort Greene and Fort Muhlenberg controlled the road to Philadelphia via King of Prussia and Gulph Mills.

Valley Forge and Monmouth to the east and Wilmington near the Head of Elk to the west were forward posts in a network of military stations and supply bases where the troops in winter quarters also had the task of preventing local foodstuffs and supplies from ships using Chesapeake Bay and the estuary of the Delaware from reaching Philadelphia.

They were connected by well-established roads with the bases in the interior. Far away at Springfield, Massachusetts was the main artillery and ordinance depot. At Albany, New York were magazines, stores, cavalry equipment, and the supplies taken from Burgoyne. Thirty miles west of the city of New York was Morristown, New Jersey, the winter quarters of the main army in the previous year, and at nearby Princeton was an army hospital. There were a number of depots in Pennsylvania including Easton on the upper Delaware with armouries and hospitals, and Allentown with its magazine. At Bethlehem thirty miles north of Valley Forge was stored the bulk of the officers' baggage and there was an important hospital manned by the Moravians. In Reading were winter quarters, hospitals and stores. At Ephrata was another hospital, at Lebanon an arsenal, and at Lancaster was a jail for Hessian prisoners. Finally, the Continental Congress, whose members were nominally in overall control of military operations, was at this time in session in the town of York to the west of the River Susquehanna. With such an imposing administrative network the soldiers in the forward posts should have been well supplied that winter, but owing to the failure of the Commissary and Quartermaster's departments, and a shortage of wagons and horses, the troops, particularly at Valley Forge, were in fact left well nigh destitute.

*

The army that reached Valley Forge from Gulph Mills on 19 December 1777 was composed of eighteen brigades of infantry, a brigade of artillery, a brigade of artificers (engineers), a brigade of local militia, three regiments of dragoons and Washington's life guards, totalling 12,000 men from eleven of the original thirteen colonies along with a few officers from South Carolina and Georgia which were not otherwise represented.

An early task at Valley Forge was to make the cabins, and the men were divided into parties of twelve and each group told to build its own hut from timber growing on the site. The huts were all made to the same specification, sixteen feet long by fourteen wide and with walls six and a half feet high. Three bunks, one above the other, were built in each corner, and since the British had destroyed the saw mill, and there were no planks available, the roofs were made of saplings covered with earth and straw. The gaps between the logs were filled with clay, the doors were formed from split slabs, and the windows were made of oiled paper when it could be had. Some groups managed to build stone chimneys but most made do with ones of wood lined with clay. A prize of twelve dollars was offered for the hut completed first in each regiment, and this reward stimulated the men's efforts considerably. As a further encouragement during the first week while they were still under canvas Washington occupied a marquee[1] in the midst of his men. The generals had huts of their own or moved into one or other of the houses in the neighbourhood. Company officers' huts were constructed in line behind those of their men, and a number of cabins of improved design were built at intervals to serve as hospitals. Washington after his first few days in the marquee made his headquarters at Isaac Potts's house near the junction of Valley Creek and the River Schuylkill. Later he built on a wooden cabin to act as a dining and conference room. The stone building next to Potts's house was used to begin with as a stable for his two horses Nelson and Blueskin. Later, however, it was converted into a hospital. Beyond was the Bake House where the ovens which baked the Revolutionary bread can still be seen in the cellars. One room[2] of the original house was used permanently for courts-martial during the army's stay. The building of the cabins was delayed by lack of horses and wagons to transport the necessary timber, but the men overcame the difficulty to some extent by yoking themselves to carriages of their own making to bring in the wood, and by 1 January 1778, the camp appears to have been nearly completed, for the Journal of the Continental Congress of that date records: 'The soldiers are nearly all covered with good huts and our camp begins to look like a spacious city.'

Although the huts provided adequate shelter, in other ways conditions at Valley Forge were deplorable. The main trouble was a shortage of food and clothing. Joseph Trumbull had managed the commissary well during the early years but he was now ill and anxious to resign and his deputies were unable to cope. Similarly Thomas Mifflin was failing as a quartermaster general. Pleading ill-health he had sent in his resignation but while his application was being considered he made no effort to discharge the duties of his office and his assistants were proving useless. The result was that the shortage of food for the men and fodder for the horses reached famine proportions. Also, to make matters worse, there was hardly any transport available for those at the camp to try and fend for themselves. As early as 21 December 1777 the only food available was meal mixed with water which the men attempted to bake into cakes. On that day, accord-

[1] Now set up in the Valley Forge Museum along with the flag Washington flew with thirteen six-point stars on a blue background.

[2] Now reconstructed in the Valley Forge Museum.

ing to Surgeon Albigense Waldo, there was a general cry through the camp: 'No meat! No meat!' After which was called out: 'What have we for dinner, boys?' and back came the answer: 'Nothing but Fire Cake and Water, Sir!' At night there were similar cries. 'Gentlemen, the supper is ready,' followed by, 'What is for supper, lads?' and the reply 'Fire Cake and Water, Sir!'

Almost as serious a problem was the shortage of shoes and clothing. On one of the early days it was reckoned that out of 11,982 in camp, 1,898 were insufficiently clad to undertake any duties whatsoever. They had to be sent to the hospital huts and neighbouring farmhouses, or be left to crouch round the fires all day.

Blistering letters about the lack of food and clothes were despatched to Congress at York, and these were couched in such strong terms that they brought a response. On 12 January Congress established a Committee of Conference to sit until further orders at Valley Forge with instructions to work out ways of improving the situation at the camp and of producing a better system of organisation and administration for the army as a whole.

The committee, often with the commander-in-chief in attendance, met almost daily for the next few months at Moore Hall two miles from head-quarters. Early on, a valuable contribution was made by the appointment at Washington's suggestion of General Greene as quartermaster general. Then, on 18 February, the committee ruled that 'provisions be laid up to support the Army: 12,000 barrels of flour near Lancaster, 8,000 near Reading and 6,000 near Bethlehem'. On 28 February, it announced that horses must be sought in Jersey, Pennsylvania and Maryland. But although such dictates, and others which followed, were later to bring good results, they did nothing to solve the immediate problems at Valley Forge. These had to be dealt with as best they could by those in the camp.

*

From the start parties were sent out into the countryside to buy and bring in any stock or provisions they could find, and on some occasions even to seize essential clothing from local inhabitants; though Washington did not really approve of doing this, as it caused so much ill feeling. As might have been expected, General Wayne took a lead in collecting what was required. On 1 March on forage in New Jersey near Haddonfield his party was all but seized by the enemy, but after a sharp skirmish, managed to return to camp with some cattle. Following this, Wayne was to report that the people of the countryside seemed to be all Tories, and it had been 'as if we were in enemy lands instead of in our own'. A week later his men

General Anthony Wayne,
engraving after John Trumbull

had another brush with the British, and had far the best of it. They inflicted several casualties and seized the 250 head of cattle the enemy had collected and added them to their own 300 head. By 27 March the situation was beginning to improve, for cattle were coming in from farther afield. On that day, droves were reported to be crossing the Delaware at Easton on their way to Valley Forge.

In January Wayne bought 650 suits of clothes from Paul Zantzinger in Lancaster for his Pennsylvanian troops, and earlier in the same month Smallwood at Wilmington managed to acquire not only clothing but also food and shoes. On 1 January the latter's troops captured an enemy sloop carrying flour, pork, poultry and other supplies. Shortly afterwards, they took the armed brig *Symmetry* after she had run aground and surrendered when two shots from a field piece were fired into her. This vessel had clothing on board for four British regiments as well as over 1,000 stand of arms, a great deal of officers' baggage, and a quantity of pork, butter and supplies: a valuable prize indeed. But there was disagreement about the distribution of the goods found in her hold, for Smallwood's officers

wanted the lot and this could not be allowed. Smallwood was also successful in bartering hides for dressed leather which he had made up into
shoes. This plan was later widely adopted, and an official rate of exchange
was fixed at five pounds of raw leather for one pound of tanned. Earlier,
Colonel Hazen while recuperating at Bethlehem had bought locally 400
pairs of shoes for his Canadians, so between them Smallwood and Hazen
were said to have 'put the Army on its feet again'.

By 23 February clothing was also beginning to arrive from outside, for
an order of the day read: 'Genl Officers are ordered to meet to arrange for
proper distribution [of clothing]. This is for the Continental Troops apart
from what the several States have supplied.' But sufficient clothing of a
uniform type was never available during the army's time at Valley Forge.
Even on 8 April 1778 Washington had perforce to write: 'We still want
for uniformity of Cloathing. We are not, like the Enemy, brilliantly and
uniformily attired. Even soldiers of the same Regiment are turned out
in various dress; but there is no excuse, as heretofore, for slovenly un-
soldierly neglect. Soldiers are to shave, have clean hands and a general air
of neatness.'

*

Early on, an ambitious programme of containment of the enemy from
Valley Forge was planned. Detachments from several brigades were
employed. Several posts north of Philadelphia were set up including one
at Gulph Mills, and parties were stationed at the fords. All had the task of
stopping people entering or leaving the city. Not as much was achieved as
had been expected, for reasons well illustrated by the following statement
made at the time: 'Instead of harassing the Enemy, we had to detach Parties to collect, if possible, as much Provision as would satisfy the present
wants of the soldiery.' But on the positive side, one reads that on 26
February, 'the Twelfth Pennsylvania guarding the roads into the City is
in daily encounter with the Enemy and his parties bent on depredation'.
Neither the militia nor the cavalry were very effective. The 1,000
Pennsylvania Militia employed to stop contact between the city and the
countryside dwindled in numbers until there were hardly any guards
within twelve miles of Philadelphia. The cavalry under Count Pulaski at
Trenton were accused of accepting bribes from local people. 'Rather than
cutting off intercourse,' it was said, 'they encourage it by suffering many
to pass who pay for it.' One cavalry leader who did consistently well,
however, was Captain Henry Lee[1]. On 16 February, he was ordered to

[1] Light Horse Harry, the father of Robert E. Lee, the commander of the Confederate
forces in the Civil War.

the Head of Elk to hasten to the army 'all the flesh and provisions in the Magazine at that place', and carried out his mission with dispatch. On another occasion, he saved himself from certain capture by his presence of mind. Surrounded at Scott's Farm near Darby by 130 British dragoons, he barricaded himself in the farmhouse and posted a corporal and four privates at different windows. When the enemy demanded his immediate surrender, he called out that Morgan's infantry were on the way and would presently cut them to pieces. Duly impressed by this information, the British withdrew; but they took with them five of Lee's troopers caught in the farm buildings.

It is clear that the American armed forces apprehended some civilians who were attempting to sell provisions to the enemy, for on 22 January at a court-martial in the Bake House several local people were sentenced for such offences. Two, it is recorded, received 'two hundred and fifty lashes on bare back, well laid on, for supplying the enemy with cattle'. Thomas Butler was found guilty of trying to carry flour into Philadelphia and received twenty lashes. Thomas Ryan, who was found guilty of trying to take 'eight quarters of mutton and a bull beef into Philada', was 'fined fifty pounds, which sum to be applied to the use of the sick at Camp'.

*

An attempt was made to run the encampment at Valley Forge on rigid, formal, military lines; but these efforts to establish an orderly, comfortable camp came to naught because of shortages of food and clothing and the severity of the weather. Undernourishment brought disease, as did the fouling of the huts by men who had no clothes to put on to visit the latrines. Also, the cold led to frost-bite. Lafayette wrote on 13 February that 'the unfortunate soldiers are in want of everything; they have neither coats, hats, shirts or shoes. Their feet and legs have frozen until they become black, and it is often necessary to amputate them'. Out of the kindness of his heart Lafayette may have been exaggerating somewhat; but two sets of established figures illustrate only too clearly the extent of the misery and suffering of the troops during their stay at Valley Forge. On 29 December—as already mentioned—not less than 1,898 men were unfit for duty from lack of clothes. In June, six months later, 3,000 had died as a result of privation and disease.

Washington, to his credit, tried hard to improve the hospital service. On 30 January 1778 he writes: 'Irregularities and disorders are reported at our hospitals in the interior parts of the State. Some sick are not tended with due care. His Excellency therefore today deputed a prudent and careful Field Officer to visit each Hospital.' The officer's duties were to draw up lists of all the sick, to make arrangements to collect the arms and accoutrements brought in by the invalids, and to transfer them to the soldiers guarding the hospitals; to ensure details were noted of the possessions of those dying in hospital; and to carry out a full inspection of the hospitals to see whether they could be improved.

Some surprising orders are found in the records of the medical services of the American army of two hundred years ago. On 7 January, Congress resolved that 'ten dollars be paid by every Officer and four dollars by every soldier who shall enter or be sent to any Hospital to be cured of venereal disease. These sums are to be deducted from the pay and shall be used for blankets, shirts and other items for sick soldiers'. On 18 April, the camp whores—who had become numerous—were ordered to serve as nurses.

*

Camp discipline which was difficult to enforce at first was tightened up when spring arrived. On 14 April appears the following: 'The Genl in his ride through Camp yesterday was pleased at the neatness, cleanliness and purity of the Camp. In some places, however, the smell was intolerable, owing to the want of Necessaries or the neglect of them. He, therefore, (and for the last time without proceeding to extremities) requests that all kinds of Dirt and Filth in front, rear and between the Hutts, or on the

Washington quelling a riot at Valley Forge

Parade, is to be raked together and burned. Regimental Quarter Masters are to see that the Necessaries which are wanted are dug immediately and that fresh earth be thrown in them every morning. Offal at the slaughter pens is to be buried. Sentinels from the Quarter Guards are to be posted at proper places who are to make prisoner any soldier who shall attempt to ease himself anywhere but at a proper Necessary. Five lashes are to be laid on immediately. This order is to be read to all soldiers and new comers immediately.'

A few months later, when the weather was warmer, orders were given for the clay closing the gaps between the logs forming the walls of the cabins to be removed in order to let in fresh air. Blank was also fired inside particularly foetid huts to fumigate them. These measures, however, appear to have been taken too late; for on 8 June comes this observation: 'The very sickly situation in Camp, and the danger of it becoming more alarming, makes it improper for the main Army to remain here . . . the Army is to take a new Camp tomorrow at 8 o'clock—this is about a mile in front of our present position. The unwholesome exhalations from the ground we occupy has made this measure necessary. We shall be at hand to take possession of our field of battle in case of any forward move on the part of the Enemy. And while we are condemned to inactivity we shall not swallow the effluvia arising from a deposit of various carcases and filth accumulated during six months.'

*

Despite the trials and tribulations of camp life, some very valuable train-ing was carried out at Valley Forge. This was made possible by the arri-val on 23 February 1778 of Baron von Steuben. Steuben, who had been recruited by Benjamin Franklin in Paris, offered his services to impart to the American army the experience he had gained serving under Frede-rick the Great in Europe. Washington had been so often disappointed by the well-recommended Europeans seeking service in the American forces that he was restrained in his welcome. He did, however, ask the newcomer to take a look at the army and give his opinion as to how its deficiencies might be remedied. After a look round Steuben announced confidently that what was required was a course of drill to instil the discipline necessary for a fighting force. This observation was so much in line with Washington's views that he was greatly impressed, and without further ado, he appointed the German an acting Inspector General with authority to organise a suitable course of training.

Steuben began by introducing a new march step which was half-way

Baron Friedrich von Steuben by
Ralph Earl

between slow and quick time and considered 'an easy natural step better than the former'. Next, he wrote out some very simple drill and musketry movements suitable for the inexperienced. When these had been translated—for he knew no English—Steuben memorised them and set about drilling the select band of 120 men who were to become his demonstration platoon. After this, one officer was chosen from each brigade to become an inspector. These Steuben gave a special course in drill and then sent back to their commands to carry the new system to the entire army. Separate squads were formed for awkward troops slow to learn the new manoeuvres, and new recruits also joined these and had to 'earn their way out by competence in the new ways'. Steuben's activities caused the greatest interest. In the first week almost the entire army—then some 5,000-strong—gathered round the drill field and became fascinated at the spectacle of the sturdy, jovial foreign general drilling the squads, giving his commands in a curious mixture of German, French and English, and roaring out multi-lingual oaths when things went wrong. The watchers also became duly impressed at the results achieved, for very soon these hours of drill produced a soldierly attitude and precision of movement which had never before been seen in the American army.

Steuben did not limit his efforts to drill. He had found 'no internal administration of any regiment in our army to his liking' and, to increase efficiency, introduced a system of inspections which he was to develop and improve on during the course of the war. Every man had to be accounted for. All articles of clothing and equipment had to be laid out periodically to be checked for serviceability and against the property account Steuben caused to be maintained in each company. He also stressed the responsibility of officers for the care of the men and the condition of their equipment. 'The captain,' he said, 'cannot be too careful of the company the State has committed to his care and should gain the love of his men by treating them with every possible kindness and humanity.'

*

On 23 April came the electrifying news of the diplomatic triumph achieved by America's three commissioners in Paris, Benjamin Franklin, Silas Deane and Arthur Lee. France had already recognised America's independence, and had sent some aid. Now she had signed a formal treaty of alliance. It seemed almost too good to be true. Surely with the support of such a powerful ally the successful conclusion of the war was assured. In any case suitable celebrations were called for; and on 6 May a great review was held in which the army was able to display its new precision at drill.

The troops paraded at nine o'clock and the procedure began by the chaplains delivering addresses of thanksgiving for the glorious news. At half-past ten a cannon was fired and the army started to assemble on the Grand Parade. According to a contemporary account:[1] 'Words cannot convey an adequate idea of the movement of the troops to their several posts; of the good order, discipline and brilliancy of their arms; and of the remarkable animation with which they performed the necessary salutes and manoeuvres.'

Washington made a circuit of the lines and was impressed with the difference between these stalwart, martial figures and the naked, starving rabble of the previous winter. When the review was over, he, along with the Marquis de Lafayette, Lord Stirling, General Greene and the other principal officers, retired to the centre of the field where an amphitheatre had been set up for an open air feast. Before this banquet took place, however, came the *feu de joie*.

The signal for it to begin was a single cannon shot fired at half-past eleven. Shortly afterwards came two more single shots and then a general

[1] Stoudt 271–274.

Benjamin Franklin, detail of
engraving after Alonzo Chappel

discharge of cannon followed by running musketry fire starting with Woodford's brigade on the right and going down the whole front line. The account continues: 'Then this fire was taken up on the left of the second line and continued to the right. The entire business was conducted with great judgement and regularity and the gradual progression of the sound from the discharge of cannon and musketry, swelling and rebounding from the neighbouring hills, gently sweeping over the Schuylkill, made military music for a soldier's ear more agreeable than the most finished pieces of Handel. After the running fire came loud huzzas: "Long Live the King of France! Long Live the friendly European Powers! Long Live the American States!"'

The *feu de joie* over, the troops were marched back to their cantonments and dismissed, after which the officers formed columns thirteen abreast, linked arms, and marched to the spot where they had been invited to have the celebration feast with the commander-in-chief. 'The amphitheatre was elegant. The outer seats were covered with tent canvas stretched on poles against the hot sun. The tables in the center were shaded by elegant marquees raised high and agreeably arranged. An excellent band played. And the feast was made still more animated by the magnanimous bearing of his Excellency and by the discourse and behaviour of the officers. Mrs. Washington, the Countess of Stirling and Lady Kitty her daughter, Mrs. Greene and other ladies, favoured the feast with their presence.' Wines and liquors circulated freely and suitable toasts were drunk including ones to the Commissioners. The account ends: 'About six the company broke up. His Excellency returned to headquarters, the officers to their billets. French officers were especially gay, particularly pleased with this public approbation of their nation. The Genl himself, in spite of fears of foreign alliances, wore a countenance of uncommon delight and complacence.'

*

On 20 April 1778 it was learnt in the British camp that Howe was going to be replaced by Clinton, which brought no comfort to the royal soldiers with whom he was far from popular. For all the criticism aimed at Howe, for all his blunders if he acted and for his indolence if he did not, he always retained an immense popularity with the men whom in the past three years he had led to victory in six battles. In spite of the ribald jokes that went around barracks about his relations with Mrs. Loring, in spite of his carousing and grafting, the men had a real affection for him. They hated to see him go, and as the time of his departure drew near felt the urge to show their feelings by some outward demonstration. A set of resolutions accompanied by a gold-headed cane or a watch and chain seemed inadequate, so, after a good deal of discussion, Captain John André, a leading light in the winter's amateur theatricals, was placed at the head of a committee with instructions to draw up plans for a farewell party in which the whole British army might participate. The result was the pageant known as *The Meschianza* which André wrote and directed. It was to prove an outstanding success.

The pageant was held on 18 May 1778 and began with a regatta, after which a procession of decorated barges with the participants aboard moved down-river from Knight's wharf to the old fort. From there they passed under two triumphal arches down a grand avenue lined with troops to the lists where mimic combat with lance, sword and pistol took place. After the mock-fighting the assembly went to a nearby mansion for dancing. Later there were fireworks on the lawn and at midnight supper was served where numerous toasts were drunk to General Howe, and, because of the affection felt for his brother, to Admiral Howe as well, although the latter was continuing to serve on the American station. After supper the dancing was resumed, and was kept up until four o'clock in the morning. The pageant passed off without incident. But only just. As the guests were leaving, cannon fire and drums beating the long roll were heard in the distance indicating that the Americans were once more in action against the abatis; and just as the last stragglers from the *Meschianza* were crawling into bed word was brought by a loyalist Quaker that General Lafayette at the head of a large body of soldiers was approaching the outposts.

*

Meanwhile, in the other camp, Washington now had nearly 12,000 men fit for duty, for although some 3,000 were lost at Valley Forge as a result of privation and disease during the winter, or desertions, in the spring, recruits had begun to pour in, particularly from Virginia. The newcomers had arrived in time to benefit from von Stenben's training with the result that Washington now possessed a formidable little army, and one moreover of high morale because of the recent alliance with France. Besides the influx of rank and file several generals had also joined for service in the field. Gates and Mifflin arrived as a result of Congress ruling that they must come directly under Washington's command. Fortunately the troubles of the period of the Conway Cabal were now over. Conway hung on in America in the hope of being reinstated, but eventually realising he was completely discredited sailed for France. Gates who had been so deeply involved, now appeared willing to cooperate fully with the commander-in-chief, so Washington confidently posted him to Peekskill. Washington also believed that Mifflin who had failed so dismally as quartermaster general would do better in the field where he had earlier shown promise. Yet another newcomer was Charles Lee. Lee who had been exchanged for General Richard Prescott arrived in the camp at Valley Forge on 23 April 1778. Washington knew nothing of the treacherous plan the captured general had prepared for Howe, and received him with full honours. The official account describes his reception as follows: 'General Lee arrived in camp. All the principal officers of the army were drawn up in two lines, advanced of the camp two miles towards the enemy. Then the troops with the inferior officers formed a line quite to headquarters. All the musick in the army attended. The General with a great number of principal officers and their suites rode about four miles on the road towards Philadelphia, and waited 'till General Lee appeared. General Washington dismounted and received General Lee as if he had been his brother. He passed through the lines of officers and the army, who all paid him the highest honours, to headquarters,[1] where Mrs. Washington was, and here he was entertained with an elegant dinner, and the musick played the whole while. A room was assigned him back of Mrs. Washington's sitting room and all his baggage was stowed in it. General Washington gave him command of the right wing of the army, and before he took charge of it, he requested to have leave to go to Congress in York Town, which was readily granted.'

From the above it would appear that the behaviour of both Washington and Lee was most correct on the occasion of the return of the latter to the American army. However, the journal of a member of Washington's household indicates that Lee was still his old self, for an entry for the day concerned reads: 'When General Lee came out this morning he looked as dirty as if he had been in the street all night. We discovered that he has brought a miserable dirty hussy with him from Philada [a British sergeant's wife] and actually took her into his room by a back door and she slept with him last night.'

*

Soon after the arrival of General Clinton in Philadelphia, ships were noticed sailing down the Delaware laden with baggage and equipment. This seemed to signify that the British were about to abandon the city, and Washington decided to make a reconnaissance in force in the direction of Philadelphia to try and find out what was happening.

On 19 May—the day after the *Meschianza*—he assembled under Lafayette a brigade of Continentals and a brigade of militia. The same day, Lafayette with his 2,000 men crossed over the Schuylkill, moved down to within ten miles of Philadelphia, and took up a defensive position at Barren Hill with outposts watching all the approach roads. Lafayette's movements which had brought him within two miles of the British outposts at Germantown were reported to the British by the Quaker whose house Lafayette had made his headquarters. Howe on being told was delighted. He felt there might very well be a chance of capturing the young French general. As this would make a pleasant leaving present, he persuaded Clinton to despatch a force to try and surround the Americans at Barren Hill.

Meanwhile, the militiamen in Lafayette's vital furthermost outpost had left their position without orders, so that warning of the enemy's approach was only given when the British brushed with a patrol near at hand on the western approach road. However, directly Lafayette realised

[1] Isaac Potts's house.

General Sir Henry Clinton

what was happening he acted with dispatch. Quickly he called in his out-posts, formed up his men, and marched them back to Matson's Ford three miles in the rear. Before the British arrived he was over the Schuylkill. He had his men deployed on the far side with his guns covering the crossing as the enemy came into sight.

When the sound of distant firing broke the silence of the dawn at Valley Forge, it took the reserve troops only fifteen minutes to get under arms; and they were soon marching to Lafayette's assistance. Long before they arrived, however, the British had decided they had missed their chance of an easy victory, and had marched back to Philadelphia.

*

Before dawn on 18 June 1778 the British army, having previously dis-patched the artillery and heavy baggage by ship to New York,[1] began to cross the Delaware and take the road for New York.

Washington had already announced to his generals his intention of fol-lowing up the British as closely as possible, of harassing them constantly,

---

[1] Along with a large number of Philadelphia Tories.

but of avoiding a set battle. On the news that the British had actually left, he sent off his army in pursuit. In the lead was Lafayette's division comprised of Woodford's, Scott's and McIntosh's brigades. It took the road for Coryell's Ferry over the Delaware, and except for a small force under Benedict Arnold left to occupy Philadelphia, the rest of the army followed, some divisions going towards Coryell's Ferry, the others to Sherard's Ferry and Easton.

Authorities differ as to the strength of Clinton's army as it marched north-east towards New York; but as he sent only a few units by sea, his total force in hand must have been something approaching 15,000. Washington's army, counting the brigades already east of the Delaware, numbered 14,500, 12,000 of whom were Continentals.

New Jersey was gripped in a heatwave. During the last week of June the temperature was over ninety degrees on every day. There were scattered thunderstorms, but these did not lower the temperature very much. It stayed muggy and was well-nigh unbearable. Because of this, and since they had also to rebuild some bridges which had been destroyed by the local militia, the British made very slow progress. The Americans having lighter packs made faster time, and on 23 June their advanced troops were within twenty miles of the British who had then reached Allentown.

At a council of war held that morning, Washington received varied advice. Lee considered they were too weak to take the offensive; Wayne, Lafayette and Greene, on the other hand, urged Washington to attack. Washington decided to do so only if a favourable opportunity presented itself.

Meanwhile, Clinton had reached Monmouth Court House, and had halted to rest his men who were suffering badly from the heat. He planned to take next day the road to Sandy Hook where he could embark his army and sail on to New York.

Directly Washington learnt of Clinton's plans, he realised his opportunity had arrived. After the main British column had left for Sandy Hook he would attack the rearguard left at Monmouth Court House with a superior force and endeavour to cut it off. Military custom demanded that Lee as next senior to Washington should be given command of the attacking force. But in view of Lee's expressed opposition to any offensive action, Lafayette was at first placed in charge. Lee, however, after some hesitation claimed his prerogative of rank, and when Lafayette graciously agreed to stand down, Washington, in the presence of the other generals, gave Lee definite orders to attack the British as they set off on the road to Sandy Hook.

At eight o'clock next morning, the British moved out with Knyphausen and his Hessians leading a long train of wagons, and Clinton and the main body in the rear. Only a small rearguard remained in the little town.

This was the moment for Lee to attack. But, although he had accepted his orders to do so the day before without hesitation, now, for some reason, he hesitated. He did nothing to prepare for an attack, and did not initiate one even after renewed orders from Washington were received next morning. He did, however, start off his troops slowly on their way towards Monmouth Court House, and then, as they approached, some of the leading brigades did launch an attack. They did not catch the British unawares, however, for the rearguard sprang to arms and drove most of the American attacking forces back again. Lee who had not wished them to attack in the first place now ordered the nearest brigade to retreat; but, rather strangely, he made no effort to see that his instructions reached the rest of his command. Soon, however, with or without orders, Lee's entire force were falling back in confusion.

Clinton now saw an opportunity of inflicting a sharp defeat on the American army. He directed Cornwallis to return with a force drawn from the rear of the column. He despatched orders to Knyphausen to send back reinforcements from the van. Pressing closely after the withdrawing Americans, Cornwallis's men soon turned the retreat into a rout. Only Wayne's brigade, falling back in good order from one delaying position to another, prevented total disaster.

Washington was at this stage at the head of the main body which was some miles behind Lee's men, and halted at rest. His first news of what was happening up in front was that Lee had received conflicting intelligence reports, but was continuing towards Monmouth Court House. On hearing this Washington was constrained to send forward reinforcements, but hesitated to do so because a number of his men were overcome by the heat—the thermometer that day reached ninety-two degrees. However, when further news arrived saying, 'the enemy is moving off at a quick pace and Genl Lee is about to attack the rearguard', Washington ordered the main body forward.

About noon, the sound of a cannon shot came from the vicinity of Monmouth Court House followed by more shots in quick succession up to a total of four or five. No answering fire, however, was audible, and not a single echo of small-arms was heard. Soon after this Henry Knox returned from the front as hot in mood as in body and reported that Lee's troops appeared to be in confusion. A civilian and an army musician were the next to arrive. They confirmed that the Continentals were in full retreat.

Washington then rode forward in some alarm. When he was passing the Freehold Meeting House he saw several columns of armed men approaching down the road. They were not in wild disorder, but staggering and exhausted, and manifestly in retreat. Behind were others, and some were coming across the fields. It seemed as if the chaos of Kip's Bay was repeating itself.

General Lee and his staff next appeared, at the head of a withdrawing column; and Washington rode up angrily to interrogate them.

'What's the meaning of this? General Lee,' he cried, 'Why all this disorder and confusion?' 'Sir, Sir?' stammered the embarrassed Lee, either not comprehending what was being asked, or disconcerted by the glint in his commander's eye. When the question was repeated, he replied that he had not thought it wise to attack, but some of his advanced troops had done so without orders. A brigade had abandoned its position and others had retired in confusion. However, all was not lost, he said. The situation was no worse than at other times when orders were not executed properly.

Washington retorted hotly that whatever Lee's opinion might be, he had expected his orders to attack to be obeyed. He must have slated Lee severely, judging by the latter's subsequent reaction; but the exact words he used are not known.

Leaving Lee still mumbling explanations, Washington now rode forward to try and right the situation. He first ordered some of the men from the retreating columns to line a hedgerow which guarded the bridge where the road crossed a stream; and impressed by their irate commander's demeanour, many left the ragged columns and went where they were directed. Next, he ordered up the main body on either side of the hedgerow defence line, Stirling's men on the left, Greene's on the right. So expeditiously were these various manoeuvres carried out, that when presently smoke and sound told of the arrival of the royal artillery on the east side of the swampy stream, four guns were ready to reply, and the whole line was prepared to receive the attack. Washington's aide, Alexander Hamilton, wrote that he never saw the General to so much advantage. 'His coolness and address were admirable,' he said. 'He instantly took measures for checking the enemy's advance, giving time for the army, which was very near, to form and make a proper disposition.'

Washington and von Steuben were now to see the results of the training carried out at Valley Forge. The Continentals stood steady, returned the British fire, and threw back one attack after another. In a final effort, Cornwallis's men reinforced by some of Knyphausen's fought their way across the swampy bed of the stream in the centre and came at the Americans with the bayonet. Even this did not daunt the Americans. Wayne quickly led them in a counter-attack, and they drove the British back. That was the end. Both sides were too worn out by the heat and the action to do more.

Washington had contemplated a full-scale assault in the morning. It was not to be. The British had marched quietly away in the night.[1] He then briefly considered pursuit, but, learning that Clinton was six hours ahead, soon realised that it was not possible to catch him up. So the British reached Sandy Hook without further interference, and from there sailed to New York. But the Americans for their part had turned a defeat into a victory; and the new army had proved its worth.

*

On 30 June 1778 Washington received a letter from Lee demanding reparation for the injury to his reputation caused by Washington's manner and words when they met near the Freehold Meeting House before the second stage of the battle. Lee said he found it incredible that Washington should have used such very singular expressions which implied that he 'was guilty of disobedience of orders, or want of conduct, or want of courage'.

Washington replied coolly to this letter which he considered in any case to have been couched in highly improper terms. He said he was not conscious of having made use of any very singular expression at the time; but that as soon as circumstances allowed, Lee could have an opportunity to explain to the Army, to Congress and America his reasons for not attacking as he had been ordered, and for making an unnecessary, disorderly and shameful retreat.

Lee sent back by return a letter seeking leave to retire from the army. Then, a few hours later, he sent another insisting on the chance of clearing himself at an immediate court of inquiry. Washington did not hesitate. He sent the Adjutant General to place Lee under arrest and to present him with charges for trial by court-martial. The court under the presidency of

[1] Official returns—probably underestimated—give some 350 casualties and some fifty heatstroke casulties for each side.

Caricature of General Charles Lee

Lord Stirling deliberated in every spare moment of time from 4 July to 9 August. Eventually Lee was found guilty on three charges: disobedience of Washington's orders to attack the enemy on 28 June; misbehaviour before the enemy by making an unnecessary, disorderly and shameful retreat; and disrespect to the commander-in-chief in his letters. He was sentenced to a year's suspension from command. When later he wrote an insulting letter to Congress, he was dismissed from the United States Army.

Meanwhile, Washington's army, after following in the wake of Clinton's, marched round to the Hudson River in the north and reinforced the blockade of New York.

Chapter Eight

MORRISTOWN

'Washington was reluctant to maintain the defensive . . . but the condition of the Army left no alternative that did not seem to him to risk too much.'

During the three years following the evacuation of Philadelphia by the British in the summer of 1778 the only military operations of note took place in the southern colonies where the British first overran Georgia and then the Carolinas. Although troops and commanders like Gates and Greene were sent to support the local forces who were contesting the British advance, Washington with the main army remained based on the Hudson Highlands and contented himself with containing the British on New York Island. Even though these years saw the arrival of French aid, Washington did not feel strong enough to do more than maintain the defensive, and it was not until the end of the period that any significant advantage was taken of the French alliance. Over the years a number of raids were successfully carried out by the Americans, but the most striking incidents of this static period of the war concerned treachery and mutiny within their ranks.

*

The first French fleet arrived off Sandy Hook on 15 July 1778. For eleven days its commander Admiral d'Estaing hung offshore, but he was not able to bring his twelve deep-laden ships inside the bight where Admiral Lord Howe's smaller fleet lay at anchor. Following this failure, an attempt was made to use temporary command of the sea to drive the British out of Newport, Rhode Island. A plan was drawn up whereby the French would put 4,000 men on to the south shore of the island while Sullivan with some 10,000 Americans made a simultaneous landing in the north. But the impetuous Sullivan crossed and landed without waiting to see whether the French were ready. Then, before d'Estaing started, Howe's fleet arrived and engaged the French ships. The resulting action

144

was indecisive but, after it had been fought, both admirals left to refit—Howe to New York, d'Estaing to Boston—leaving Sullivan to do the best he could on his own. He very soon decided to withdraw, and after fighting a spirited rearguard action in the north of the island managed to get away; but he had suffered some 200 casualties, killed, wounded and missing, and all to no purpose.

After refitting at Boston Admiral d'Estaing sailed for the West Indies, and Washington continued the blockade of New York on his own. The disposition of the American forces at this time was as follows: Putnam was at West Point, New York; Gates was at Danbury, Connecticut; Stirling at Mahopak, New York; and Washington with the main army was at Middlebrook, New Jersey. Washington's object in making these dispositions was to safeguard the bases in the Hudson Highlands and protect his communications with New England and the Southern colonies.

No operations of any magnitude occurred in New Jersey during that winter or the following spring, but in June 1779 word came that the British were moving north and approaching King's Ferry which linked the unmanned Stony Point on the west bank of the river with an American post at Verplancks on the east bank. The important crossing was only twelve miles from West Point which was now Washington's main bastion guarding the Hudson Highlands. He had been anxious to retain the two posts, not only to safeguard the crossing, but also to prevent the enemy from approaching West Point, and was, therefore, distressed to learn a few days later that the small American garrison at Verplancks had surrendered and that the enemy had occupied Stony Point and begun to fortify it, as if to remain there permanently. Washington soon decided that Clinton's move into the Hudson Highlands would have to be countered, and he thought he possessed the right weapon to achieve this in a newly formed light infantry brigade under Anthony Wayne. Without delay, a thorough reconnaissance was carried out in the neighbourhood of the two posts; and finally it was decided that a surprise night attack would be the best method of recapturing Stony Point, and that Wayne and his 13,000 men of the light infantry brigade should be allotted the task of carrying it out.

On the morning of 15 July 1779 Wayne paraded his men 'fresh shaven and well powdered' at Sandy Beach thirteen miles from Stony Point, and afterwards led them off towards his objective. Following a long march, he halted them a mile short of Stony Point to issue his final orders. These were short and to the point. All except the men of one battalion who were to create a diversion by musket fire would march with empty muskets and bayonets fixed. Until the final assault silence would be absolute. Then all would shout loudly, 'The fort's our own!'

At midnight Wayne's force started to cross the swamp, moving forward in two columns with axe-men ahead to cut pathways through the abatis and 'forlorn hopes' ready to rush through the first passable gap. In spite of the attempts at silence an alert British picket heard the confused squelching in the swamp and at his alarm the garrison sprang to arms. Then came the roar of musketry from between the advancing American columns. This had the desired effect, causing the British commander to lead half his force in the direction of the firing, and so thinning his flanks that both columns were able not only to hack their way through the abatis largely unhindered, but to climb the parapet, and to force their way, yelling as they fought, right through to the citadel.

Heavily outnumbered, and bewildered by the Americans' continuous cries of 'the fort's our own', all the fight then went out of the British. Up in the log barracks a party from the 17th Regiment held out for a time, but all eventually capitulated. In thirty minutes of impetuous assault Wayne had won Stony Point and had taken revenge for his defeat at Paoli. He had also earned his soubriquet 'Mad Anthony'.

As soon as Stony Point had been taken, the guns of the fort were opened on the supporting warship at anchor on the river; but hurriedly slipping her cable the sloop dropped down-stream out of range. Next fire was directed on the post at Verplancks opposite. It had been planned that Robert Howe's force should attack Verplancks directly Stony Point was captured; but no Americans could be seen on the far bank. In fact Howe unlike Wayne had shown little enterprise. Having served only two months with the main army, he was largely unfamiliar with the countryside and when he lost his way gave up long before he reached his objective. However, his failure being tacitly ignored, there was great rejoicing over the dramatic seizure of Stony Point. The army was naturally cock-a-hoop at the news, and a gratified Congress extended a vote of thanks to Washington and Wayne.

*

One of the effects of the raid was to encourage other leaders to try and do likewise. Only one month later Major Henry Lee sought permission to try and seize the British post at Powles Hook on the west bank of the Hudson opposite the lower end of New York Island. Lee had earlier been the cause of embarrassment to Washington. Just before the attack on

Stony Point the British had raided and damaged New Haven, Connecticut and burned to the ground the neighbouring towns of Fairfield and Norwalk. Washington wanted to make these outrages known to the world, but was restrained because of a gruesome incident in his own army. Lee had suggested to Washington that desertion might be discouraged if the culprits were hanged immediately and their decapitated heads sent to the camps. The general replied that he endorsed summary execution in the circumstances, but thought it better not to cut off the heads of deserters. 'Examples,' he said, 'however severe, ought not to be attended with an appearance of inhumanity.' Before this letter reached Lee, however, he had carried out his threat and hanged and decapitated a runaway. Washington was shocked. He remonstrated with Lee and concluded: 'You will send and have the body buried lest it fall into enemy hands.' It was not necessary to tell Lee what the British would make of such an incident in answer to charges that they had been cruel in the raids on the Connecticut coast. Stunned as Washington had been, however, he did not discard Lee or lose faith in him. One blunder did not presuppose another. Therefore after pointing out the dangers of an attack on Powles Hook, and stressing the importance of surprise, he told Lee the attempt might be made if he could get the approval of Lord Stirling who commanded in that district.[1]

Stirling's approval was in due course granted and on 18 August 1779 Lee set out for Powles Hook at the head of 400 men. They started from New Bridge on the Hackensack River on an advance that would not bring them down to the area of probable enemy patrol until night had fallen. The troops were to assemble in the area between Bergen and the marshes bordering Powles Hook, and were to launch their attack in the early hours of the morning.

On reaching the assembly point, after being delayed by an unsatisfactory guide, it was reported that nearly half the Virginian contingent was missing. This was bad news indeed, for Lee required every bayonet, and he paused for a few moments to consider what he should do. Then an officer sent forward to reconnoitre returned to say that he had found the fort silent and although its protective ditch was nearly full of water it could be easily forded by the bridge. Lee hesitated no longer. He advanced his men in two columns with 'forlorn hopes' ahead, and by four o'clock in the morning they had reached the ditch at the recommended place. At a whispered word, they plunged in, splashing noisily as they

[1]   16 G.W. 82–84, 217–18.

Major Henry Lee by Alonzo Chappel

headed for the opposite bank. All had been silent in the fortifications during the approach march, but now from behind the abatis came the shout of a sentinel and a warning shot. Before, however, the garrison could spring to arms, Lee's men were hacking their way through the abatis and breaking in to the main works. They were inside in time to surprise and surround the men emerging to take up their action stations, and the poor dazed defenders trickling out in small groups could only stop and raise their startled hands in surrender. The British commander at the head of some Hessians contrived to hold out in a blockhouse; but as fifty enemy had already been bayoneted and three times that number made prisoner, Lee felt he had achieved his aim. Further delay might result in being trapped with muskets useless because the powder had been wetted crossing the ditch. There was no time to deal with the diehards in the blockhouse; nor to spike the enemy guns. A plan to burn the barracks was discarded because women and children were inside. So, herding his prisoners before him, Lee set off on his way back. It had been intended to march over to the Hackensack where barges would be waiting to take them across to the relative safety of the far shore, but when they arrived at the river no vessels could be seen, and the tired men had to retrace their steps to Bergen and take the road between the rivers for New Bridge. On the way home they were joined by the defecting Virginians and a detachment sent down by Lord Stirling to support them. This was fortunate as, with their dry powder, these two groups were able to drive off some Tories coming back from a foraging party who threatened them. Thus it came about that at one o'clock in the afternoon after a gruelling march the entire command reached New Bridge safely along with all the prisoners.

Lee had been very lucky. Failure to keep his column together, to assure his men had dry powder, and to make certain the boats were at the chosen spot might have ruined the operation. Washington, however, did not point out Lee's omissions. It had been an inspiring exploit and one which would raise the spirits of the whole American army. The commander-in-chief therefore highly commended Lee in General Orders and in a dispatch to Congress. In due course Congress was to award Lee a medal and to provide a handsome sum of dollars to distribute among his men.

*

For the winter of 1779–80 Washington chose Morristown in which to quarter his Continental regiments. The area selected for the main camp was three miles south-west of the village of Jockey Hollow; Washington made his headquarters at the mansion of a widow named Mrs. Theodosia Ford in the village itself; his life guards occupied an open space directly opposite; and the artillery park was placed a mile west of headquarters. The bulk of the troops reached Morristown during the first week of December 1779 and the rest arrived before the end of the month. Estimates vary as to their total effective strength but there were probably not under 10,000 men nor over 12,000. Eight infantry brigades recruited from Pennsylvania, New York, Maryland and Connecticut occupied Jockey Hollow, and a New Hampshire brigade and one from New Jersey were assigned camping grounds nearby.

Directly the men arrived they pitched their tents on the frozen snow, and then began to build log huts to house themselves. This proved difficult, for although there was ample oak, walnut and chestnut timber at hand, the men were handicapped by early snowstorms and bitter cold. In spite of this, however, an imposing log-house city was eventually created.

Weather conditions when the army arrived at Morristown were but a foretaste of what was yet to come, for as things turned out 1779–80

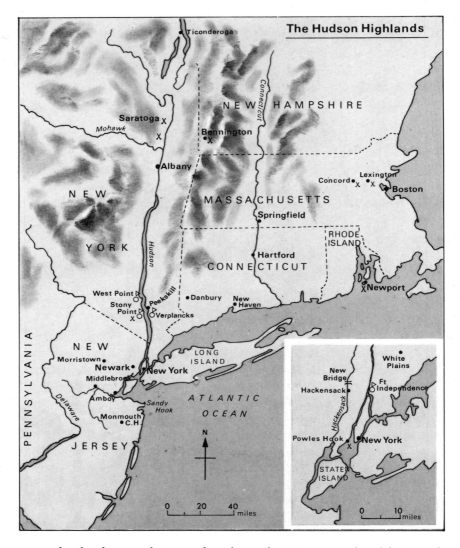

proved to be the most bitter and prolonged winter not only of the Revolutionary War but of the whole eighteenth century. One observer recalled four snowfalls in November, seven in December, six in January, four in February, six in March and one in April, twenty-eight altogether. The great storm of 2–4 January 1780, before all the huts had been built, was among the most memorable on record, with high winds which no man could endure many minutes without danger to his life. 'Several marquees were torn asunder and blown down over the officers' heads in the night,' wrote Dr. Thacher, 'and some of the soldiers were actually covered while in their tents, and buried like sheep under the snow.' When this blizzard finally subsided the snow lay full four feet deep on a level and drifted in places to six feet or more, filling up the roads, covering the tops of fences, and making it practically impossible to travel anywhere with heavy loads. What made things worse was the intense, penetrating cold. General Greene noted that for a week in January no one could leave their huts because of it. Only on one day that month did the mercury go above freezing point. All the rivers froze solid including both the Hudson and the Delaware, so that troops and even large cannon could pass over them. Ice in the Passaic River formed three feet thick and as late as 26 February the Hudson above New York was 'full of ice on the banks and floating ice in the channel'. The Delaware remained wholly impassable to navigation for three months. 'The oldest people now living in the country,' wrote Washington on 18 March, 'do not remember so hard a winter as the one we are now emerging from.'

The misery caused by the cold was added to by the chronic shortage of clothes, blankets and footwear and also by shortages of food for the men and fodder for the transport animals. At the end of February General Greene was to write: 'Our provisions are in a manner gone; we have not a ton of hay at command nor magazines to draw from.' On 25 March Washington records: 'The army is now upon a most scanty allowance, and is seldom at the expiration of one day certain of a morsel of bread for the next.'[1] To add to the troubles there was a shortage of money to pay the men, and the little available was in Continental paper currency worth less than a fortieth part of hard coin. This made it difficult to retain the men in camp and also to recruit replacements. In spite of all these difficulties thanks to the exertions of the few officers who remained at Morristown desertion at first remained at a low figure, but as the savage weather grew fiercer discipline deteriorated, desertions grew in numbers, and finally there was the mutiny of two Connecticut regiments in Jockey Hollow. This was quickly suppressed but it foreshadowed the more serious out-bursts which were to come within a year.

Although his army was in such poor shape that winter, Washington

[1] 18 G.W. 150.

nevertheless managed to stage a number of raids against enemy positions. The most significant of these occurred when in the middle of January 1780 Stirling raided Staten Island at the head of a force of some 3,000 men, by crossing over to the island on five hundred sleighs. His object was to capture as much enemy material as possible, but unfortunately the British heard about the proposed raid and were able to retire in time into their defence posts where they could defy attack. The result was that Stirling's force after spending a miserable twenty-four hours in the snowbound countryside were only able to bring off a handful of provisions, blankets and stores. An unfortunate feature of the venture was the misconduct of a number of New Jerseymen who having joined the expedition in the guise of militiamen spent their time on the island plundering the farms. All the stolen property that could be recovered was returned a few days later, but much serious harm was done to public relations.

On 19 April there was an interesting event to break the monotony of camp life when the French minister made a call on the American army. The highlight of the visit was described by Dr. Thacher as follows: 'A field of parade being prepared under the direction of the Baron Steuben, four battalions of our army were presented in review by the French minister . . . thirteen cannon, as usual, announced his arrival . . . a large stage was erected in the field which was crowded by officers, ladies and gentlemen of distinction from the country, among whom were Governor Livingston of New Jersey and his lady. Our troops exhibited a truly military appearance, and performed the manoeuvres and evolutions in a manner which afforded much satisfaction to our commander-in-chief, and they were honored by the approbation of the French minister and by all present . . . in the evening General Washington and the French minister attended a ball provided by our principal officers, at which were present a numerous collection of ladies and gentlemen of distinguished character. Fireworks were also exhibited by the officers of the artillery.' The French minister was able to assure them that other French fleets and a body of troops were on their way and this happy news was reaffirmed a month later when Lafayette arrived at the camp at Morristown after a year's absence in France. A few months later the French fleets along with 5,000 troops duly arrived, but it was nevertheless nearly a year before advantage[1] began to be made of the French alliance.

Early in June less welcome news arrived. Reports reached camp that the enemy had taken Charleston, capturing General Lincoln and his entire

[1] The real advantage was of course taken at Yorktown in 1781.

army of 5,000 men. At the same time it was learnt that a force under General von Knyphausen had invaded New Jersey and was starting to march towards Morristown. The Continental army had lost the Maryland brigades which had been sent south to contest Cornwallis's advance through the Carolinas and also the New York brigade which had left for the Hudson Highlands, but Washington moved forward those troops that still remained at Morristown to meet the British invaders. After a brush near Springfield the British fell back to the coast, and for two weeks the two sides remained watching each other. Then the Americans became even more concerned by a greater threat to their advanced position at Morristown when it was learnt that Sir Henry Clinton and the force that had captured Charleston had returned to New York and was available for local adventures.

The knowledge of Clinton's return caused Washington to remove the bulk of his military stores from Morristown to less vulnerable bases in the interior. After detailing a small force under Greene to watch Knyphausen's men, he also moved the rest of the army north to Rockaway Bridge and Pompton from where they could equally well protect Morristown or West Point from attack.

On 23 June, the very day of Washington's departure north from Morristown, Knyphausen advanced again and burnt most of the buildings in Springfield. However, after this he met with such spirited resistance from Greene's force that he withdrew again, first to the coast and then back over to Staten Island. Directly Washington felt assured that the threat in this quarter had been removed, he marched his troops north towards the Hudson Highlands, choosing as the station for the main body of his Continentals the town of New Windsor situated on the west branch of the Hudson a few miles north of West Point. Here the bulk of the army was to have its encampment during the autumn of 1780 and the winter of 1780–81, though the New Jersey Line was assigned quarters at Pompton midway between West Point and Middlestown, and ten infantry regiments and one artillery regiment of the Pennsylvania Line returned and occupied some of the log huts built at Jockey Hollow for the winter of 1779–80.

Chapter Nine

WEST POINT

'Lafayette thought that Arnold's idea must have been to invite the enemy
to move in and then pretend to be taken by surprise.'

During the autumn of 1780 Washington was to lose in very strange circumstances the services of one of his best generals. Having come to the
conclusion that no immediate attack on the enemy on New York Island
was possible, Washington had set about the task of making certain that his
fortification on the Hudson, particularly those at West Point, were strong
enough to discourage an attack by the British. He felt confident that the
key defences on the river were being strengthened by his energetic subordinate Benedict Arnold; but wishing to see the state of affairs for himself,
on 23 September 1780 he took the road to West Point making for the
home of Beverley Robinson, on the east bank of the Hudson and two
miles from the fortress, which Arnold was using as his headquarters.

Washington and his staff arrived at their destination about 10.30 in the
morning, and were met by a junior aide who, full of embarrassment,
attempted to explain why his master was not able to greet the commander-in-chief in person. While at breakfast, the aide said, Arnold had
received an urgent call to go across the river to West Point. He would be
back in about an hour and in the meantime Lieutenant Colonel Varick
was on his way to meet them. The aide added that Mrs Arnold had
recently had a child and was confined to her room, but that the necessary
arrangements for a meal for the commander-in-chief and his staff had
been made.

In due course Varick arrived and after breakfast at which the senior staff
officer played the host, as there was still no sign of Arnold, Washington
and his officers had themselves rowed over to West Point. Washington
expected to find Arnold at the landing, but he was not there, nor had he
been seen that morning by those who greeted the visitors. Washington
concluded that the missing general was at one of the defences where per-

haps some problem of construction had arisen. He decided to start on his inspection and go from one work to another until Arnold was found. As he made his rounds, he encountered shocking conditions of past bad planning and of present neglect. Some of the forts had not been completed and others had fallen into disrepair, most of the bundles of fascines were so dry as to be easily set alight, and many *chevaux de frise* were broken. Strangely enough, very few men were visible either as guards or at work on the fortifications.

At each of the forts Washington inquired after Arnold, but nobody had seen him. The commander of one post indeed declared that so far as he knew Arnold had not set foot there during the morning. Washington felt some irritation that an officer of Arnold's experience should be absent when forewarned of a visit, but as it was important to know the exact condition of the defences, he continued with his tour. The full inspection took so long that it was well past three o'clock when Washington and his staff started back across the river, and close to four o'clock before they reached Robinson's landing; but even after so long an absence Arnold had not returned. It was very strange.

Benedict Arnold from Washington Irving's biography of Washington

A little later, when Washington was in his room changing his clothes,

Alexander Hamilton came in bearing a bulky packet of papers which he said he thought should have the commander-in-chief's personal attention. The packet had been brought in by the commander of the dragoons, and an explanatory note said it had been found on a man calling himself John Anderson who had been captured in suspicious circumstances on the road to New York.

The papers were interesting indeed. There was an officer's pass for John Anderson dated 22 September, a summary of the army's strength, a report on the troops at West Point, a return of ordnance, the arrangements for the disposition of artillery at an alarm, a description of the works at West Point, and a copy of the minutes of a recent important council of war that Washington had sent to Arnold a few days previously: in short, a dossier of some of the most confidential papers concerning the strength of the army and the state of the defences of West Point. This was startling enough. What was quite appalling was that two papers were unmistakably in Arnold's handwriting. There was also enclosed in the packet a letter addressed to Washington which was evidently written in case of capture, for it explained succinctly the whole matter. It seemed the arrested man was not John Anderson but Major André; and he had left the *Vulture* in the Hudson River to meet someone 'who had something important to tell him'. Having done his business he had not been allowed to go back to his ship in uniform and had been compelled to disguise himself and start off for New York on foot. He begged that a message might be sent to General Clinton explaining his predicament.

Washington was deeply shocked to realise that André had been given the incriminating documents by Arnold himself. But he gave no outward indication of his state of mind and merely ordered the British officer to be kept in custody while he continued his enquiries into Arnold's movements earlier in the day. Concerning this, he was told that while Arnold was having breakfast a paper was brought in whose contents upset him, and after stuffing it in his pocket, he got up and left the table. In retrospect this was suspicious, for it must have been a warning. Arnold must have fled, and, if so, had doubtless gone off to find the vessel from which Major André had come ashore. Jumping to his feet, Washington called for Alexander Hamilton and told him to take horse and try and intercept the fugitive. Then he calmly completed his toilet in preparation for dinner.

When the meal was over, Washington asked Varick to get his hat and come for a walk, and as they strolled along together, Washington told Arnold's chief staff officer about his master's conduct. Varick was aghast at the news, and immediately began to disclose all he knew about Arnold. He recalled that he had first been puzzled and then troubled when he discovered that Arnold was having dealings with Joshua Hett Smith who he had good reason to believe was a spy and trader in illicit enemy goods, and he also related how concerned he had been about several unexplained journeys made by Arnold down-river.

Soon after Washington got back to the house, he was told that her husband's flight seemed to have caused Mrs Arnold to take leave of her senses, for she had been raving all day as if insane. When it was attempted to comfort her by saying he would return, she had cried, 'He is gone, gone forever!' Now she was calling frantically for General Washington and demanding that he should come and see her. Washington went with Lafayette and Varick to her room and found her in a very distressed state. Her hair was down and her clothing in disarray. She kept walking up and down weeping profusely, sometimes with her baby in her arms. She did not recognise Washington and declared he was a man who had come to kill her child. Obviously unable to help in any way, Washington soon left; but he was relieved to learn next morning that she had shaken off her hysteria, and was asking to be allowed to return to the home of her Tory parents in Philadelphia. As there seemed no reason why she should be held at West Point, Washington allowed her to leave, one of Arnold's aides being detailed as escort.

Washington's next task was to set about strengthening the defences of West Point against a possible British attack, for it was obvious that Arnold must have purposely scattered his garrison in order to weaken resistance to the enemy. Two hundred men had been detailed as woodchoppers and others had been placed where they would be useless or could be cut off. Those who remained had no posts assigned them nor had they been given a single order as to what to do if attacked. Lafayette suggested that Arnold's idea must have been to invite the enemy to move in, and then pretend he had been taken by surprise and overwhelmed; and Washington was inclined to agree.

To rectify Arnold's omissions, the wood-cutting party was recalled, the north and middle redoubts were fully manned, Greene was ordered to advance a division to King's Ferry, and the main army was put on short call. Then, as soon as these arrangements were carried out, Washington took up again the task of getting to the bottom of the Arnold affair.

As a first step, he arrested Joshua Hett Smith whom Varick had earlier described as a suspect. Smith immediately began to protest against the arrest of so loyal an American citizen, and being extremely voluble it took some time to bring him to a state of mind in which he would answer questions without making a speech. Eventually, however, he did produce a few facts that filled some of the gaps in Washington's knowledge of the affair. He said that at Arnold's insistence, he had rowed down-stream and visited the *Vulture* with instructions to bring back Colonel Beverley Robinson for an interview with Arnold; but that in the event he had been told to take John Anderson instead. When Washington asked why it had been decided to send Arnold's visitor back by land, Smith replied that he had caught a fever and had not been well enough at the time to row Anderson back. Washington and his staff next began the exhausting task of going through Arnold's papers. From these came further confirmation of the missing general's treachery; but there was one consolation; even though they went carefully through the traitor's correspondence, they were unable to find any other member of the garrison involved. The only other American on whom the correspondence cast the faintest shadow of suspicion was Joshua Hett Smith.

*

After the investigation into Arnold's affairs had been completed Washington returned to the main army encampment at Tappan along with André and Hett Smith under armed guard; and on arrival at Tappan Washington received a message from Clinton pleading that André should not be treated as a spy but be granted permission to return unharmed. Having decided, however, that as André had been caught in civilian clothes he must be treated as a spy, Washington would not agree to the British commander's request, and instead, appointed a board of officers to make 'a candid and speedy recommendation of the case', in confidence that his subordinates would come to the same conclusion as himself.

André, when questioned, confessed openly the full purpose of his visit and his involvement in the plan to persuade a disgruntled Arnold to facilitate the occupation of the fortress and change sides. The captured British officer was so open about all his activities and possessed such youthful charm that the board was greatly upset that 'so gallant an officer and so accomplished a gentleman' should end his career on the gallows; but knowing Washington's views on the matter and accepting the undoubted fact that André had gone to see Arnold secretly, and then had returned 'in a disguised habit' carrying documents containing secret information, the board eventually came to the unanimous decision that André ought to be considered 'a spy from the enemy', and that in accordance with the law and usage of nations he ought to suffer death.

Having received the report of the board Washington sent a copy to

Major John André, self-portrait

Clinton by way of an answer to his letter, and he added the following words: 'From the proceedings it is evident that Major André was employed in the execution of measures very foreign to the objects of flags of truce and such as were never meant to authorize or countenance in the most distant degree; and that as this gentleman confessed with the greatest candor in the course of his examination, it is impossible for him to suppose he came on shore under the sanction of a flag.'

*

The last moments of the young officer were harrowing in the extreme. André partook of a breakfast sent from Washington's table which had served him daily. Then he shaved and dressed himself in his scarlet coat and buff breeches, though he did not put on his sash or sword. After that he laid his hat on the table and said to his officer escorts who had now entered his room, 'I am ready at any minute, gentlemen, to wait on you.' When the procession started a large number of officers rode in front of the wagon that contained the black-painted coffin. Behind walked André with an officer on either side locked arm in arm with his. In silence stepping to the drum, the prisoner and guards walked along the old Tappan road until they came to the turn up the hill to the gallows. The moment André saw the gibbet he stopped and stared, for he had requested to be shot not hanged. Asked what was wrong, he said, 'Must I die in this manner?' When he was told it was unavoidable, he replied. 'I am reconciled to my fate but not to the mode.' Then he marched stiffly on.

At the place of execution there was a brief agonizing wait during which André looked up several times at the gibbet, abstractedly rolling a small stone under the sole of one of his shoes while he swallowed hard. When the wagon was placed under the gallows he quickly climbed into it and stood on his coffin. Once again he recoiled, but consoled himself audibly, 'It will be but a momentary pang.' Then he deliberately prepared his neck for the noose by opening his collar and untying his stock. When the executioner tried to put the rope under his chin, André pushed the man back, adjusted the rope, put the queue of his hair outside it, and bandaged his own eyes. Colonel Scammell read the death warrant, and concluded, 'Major André, if you have anything you wish to say more, you now have the opportunity.' André pulled up the handkerchief that covered his eyes and replied, 'Nothing, but to request you will witness to the world that I die like a brave man.' Then when the Provost Marshal told him his hands must be pinioned, he took out another handkerchief and passed it to the officer. When the wagon was pulled away, André's body swung violently in the air. He struggled a little but death appeared almost instantaneous. The corpse was not cut down for twenty minutes or so.

*

The reasons for Benedict Arnold's change of side appear to have been complex. To begin with he was no doubt influenced by his wife whose sympathies were with the British. Then he considered he had been shabbily treated by Congress during the early years of the war by not being offered appointments worthy of his talents. Finally, when military governor in Philadelphia after the British left in 1778, charges had been brought before Congress concerning some high-handed actions of his; in due course he had been reprimanded for his behaviour, which had upset

The execution of Major André, engraving by M. A. Wageman

him considerably. After Arnold had gone over to the enemy he was appointed the leader of a British expedition into Virginia, and this he was in the process of conducting vigorously about the time that Cornwallis was entering Virginia from the south.

*

The winter of 1780–81 was spent by the main army at New Windsor, by the New Jersey line at Pompton and by the Pennsylvania line at Jockey Hollow near Morristown in New Jersey. Morale during this period was extremely low throughout the American army; and especially among the Pennsylvanians in New Jersey. Not only did these troops lack clothing and blankets but they were without a drop of rum to fortify themselves against the piercing cold. Another complaint concerned pay, for late-comers were being given enhanced bounties while many first-comers, their smaller bounties spent, had not seen even a paper dollar in pay for over twelve months. The major trouble, however, was about the interpretation of the terms of enlistment. Many soldiers considered their enlistment 'for three years, or during the war' entitled them to be discharged at the end of three years or sooner if the war ended earlier, and declared that their officers, by claiming their enlistments ran as long as the war lasted, were unjustly holding them beyond the agreed time.

Anthony Wayne had known for a long time that his men would make trouble if their grievances were not remedied and had repeatedly urged the authorities in Pennsylvania to do something. His entreaties fell on deaf ears, and on 1 January 1781 almost the whole Pennsylvania line, having turned out by prearrangement, seized the artillery and ammunition, and prepared to leave camp. In a vain attempt to restore order, one officer was killed and two others were wounded, and even the popular Wayne, although he bravely rode in among them, could not persuade the mutineers to lay down their arms. At eleven o'clock that night they marched off towards Philadelphia with the announced intention of laying their case before Congress.

It was not until five days after the outbreak of the mutiny that Washington received from Wayne the first details of what had occurred. The troops, Wayne reported, had reached Princeton and he had opened negotiations with a committee of sergeants the mutineers had appointed to act for them. He also said that a paper had been handed to him in which it was demanded that discharges be granted to those entitled to them, that arrears of pay and clothing be made up, and that participants in the revolt be exempt from punishment. Wayne expressed the view that the authorities of Pennsylvania should be left to deal with 'this unhappy business' and said that Washington would be well advised to keep away.

Replying to Wayne's dispatch in a letter dated 8 January Washington said that although he was not averse to a generous settlement he thought a bargain should not be made which might be dangerous to the rest of the army 'who are nearly in the same condition'. However, he followed Wayne's suggestion and stayed away.

On 9 January came the disturbing news that the British had sent a commissioner to the mutineers offering them generous terms if they changed sides; but this was followed almost immediately by a dispatch saying that the sergeants had made the agent their prisoner. Washington now called a council of war at West Point to decide what should be done. After a lengthy discussion and in spite of vigorous opposition from General Heath, it was decided to form a detachment of 1,000 reliable troops to be ready to move south if circumstances required.

Meanwhile, representatives from Congress and the State of Pennsylvania had come to Princeton to negotiate. After a brief discussion most of the demands of the mutineers were met. Enlistments for three years or the duration of the war were to be considered as expiring at the end of the third year; shoes, linen overalls and shirts were promised shortly; and back pay was to be provided forthwith. Commissioners appointed by Congress were then set to work at once on the details, and as a result of a settlement on the above terms, half the mutineers were released from the army and the rest were allowed to go on furlough for several months. One welcome result was that once their main grievances had been removed a large number re-enlisted.

*

Washington appears to have been relatively happy with the outcome. Writing to Rochambeau at Newport he said: 'These men, however lost to a sense of duty, had so far retained that of honor as to reject the most advantageous proposition from the enemy . . . the rest of the army (the Jersey troops excepted) . . . I would flatter myself will continue to struggle under the same difficulties they have hitherto endured which I cannot help remarking seem to reach the bounds of human patience.'[1]

The above was written on 20 January 1781 when Washington had no grounds, so far as is known, for regarding the reference to the Jersey troops as more than a casual statement of fact. But the very next day, he found himself a vindicated prophet of evil, for Colonel Israel Shreve reported that some of those identical Jersey soldiers then in camp at Pompton had mutinied and were marching towards Trenton. 'They have lately received a part of their pay,' 'Shreve, 'and most of them are much disguised with liquor.'

Were all the Jersey troops involved? Was this uprising in concert with that of the Pennsylvanians part of a movement that was to spread from one command to another until the army was destroyed? Washington did not wait to find out. This time there would be no negotiations by civil authority, no temporizing, no compromise. If the best soldiers of the army would stand by him, he would march with them and quell the mutiny. As quickly as dispatches could be drafted and copied they were signed and sent out. Shreve at Pompton was to collect all the regiments who he thought would not follow 'the pernicious example of their associates'. If Shreve had then the necessary strength he was to compel the soldiers in revolt to return to duty. Meanwhile, Heath at West Point was to pick five or six hundred of the 'most robust and best clothed' men of the citadel's garrison, and was to place them under proper officers at once. Washington himself would be at West Point the next morning to inspect them. Help was also sought from John Sullivan who had recently retired from the army on account of ill-health and had become a member of

---

[1] 21 G.W. 119–20.

Congress. Sullivan was informed of the danger and tactfully asked to oppose intervention by Congress, for, said Washington: 'This spirit of mutiny will spread itself through the remainder of the army if not extinguished by some decisive measure. I shall as quick as possible, at all events, march a detachment to compel the mutineers to submission, and I beg leave strongly to recommend that no terms may be made with them.'[1]

The next day, having ridden to West Point, Washington placed Robert Howe in command of the detachment with explicit instructions to compel the mutineers to unconditional submission, and adding, 'I am to desire you will grant no terms while they are with arms in their hands in a state of resistance. The manner of executing this I leave to your discretion according to circumstances. If you succeed in compelling the revolted troops to surrender you will instantly execute a few of the most active and incendiary leaders.'[2]

Washington was convinced that unless the mutiny was quickly suppressed a spirit of insubordination would spread throughout the whole army. His strongest reassurance in making the gamble of using force to stamp out the insurrection was that most of Howe's troops would be drawn from New England.

Howe was slow to get started as a heavy snowstorm on 23 January made travelling conditions impossible, but by 26 January when the snow was packed smoothly enough for sleighing he marched his detachment to Pompton. By dawn on 27 January he had placed his men and his guns in a position that commanded the huts in which the mutineers were asleep. After that, if the gunners did their duty and the infantrymen would aim and fire, the mutineers could be slaughtered to the last skulker. Howe then directed a senior officer to make a round of the camp, and to order the Jersey troops to parade without arms and to march to a place he would designate.

The response from the mutineers who came streaming out of their huts rubbing the sleep from their eyes was mixed. Some complained that more specific conditions for surrender should have been offered; others seemed ready to do as they were told. Howe's next step was to move his men and his cannon up to point-blank range, after which he sent word that the mutineers had only five minutes to decide. The crisis was now at hand. On it hung the outcome of the Jersey mutiny, its spread, and, perhaps, the continuance of the army in the field. If the men in the huts remained defiant

[1] 21 G.W. 128.
[2] 21 G.W. 128.

and the soldiers of the detachment refused to pull triggers, it might be the end of everything. Tense seconds of waiting followed. Then the mutineers who had returned to their huts reappeared, bundled up for the snow but without arms, and formed up on the parade ground under the guns of Howe's detachment.

Howe by this time had consulted the Jersey officers and discovered the names of the ringleaders of the mutiny, including the three most violent. These latter were brought immediately before a field court-martial who speedily condemned them to death.

The execution that followed was a gruesome affair. Howe sought from the Jersey officers the twelve names of the next most active of the mutineers and sent them back to the huts for their muskets. On their return they were divided into two parties of six and formed up as a firing squad in front of the first victim, a sergeant, who was made to kneel before them. Howe's instructions were explicit. One party was to fire first, three at the head and three at the heart. If the man was not then dead, the second party was to fire. And let them protest and weep if they will. They were lucky not to be in the sergeant's place.

Fire! Still in spasm. Fire, you second party. He is dead. Now the next villain. Load for him. Proceed as before. Good! Dead on the first discharge. Now for the third. What? Are the Jersey officers interceding on his behalf. Was he, as they say, forced into leadership, and was endeavouring all the while to persuade the mutineers to return to their duty? Perhaps so. Reprieve him, then. General Washington will pass finally on his case.[1]

When it was all over, the rest were marched off the field and paraded by regiments under their own officers whom they would have to acknowledge to obey for the future. 'I then spoke to them by platoons,' Howe said later, 'representing to them in the strongest terms I was capable of, the heinousness of their guilt as well as the folly of it . . . they thereupon . . . showed such strong marks of contrition that I think I may pledge myself for their future good conduct.'[2]

Washington received Howe's report with deep relief, and fully endorsed everything the general had done. On 7 February following, he ordered the New Jersey Brigade to Morristown to take up as their quarters the huts previously occupied by the disintegrated Pennsylvania line. They remained so posted until 8 July 1781 when they returned to the

[1] Thacher 252.
[2] 7 Sparks 564–65.

Hudson.

While this was happening in the vicinity of New York Island, the tide of war in the South was moving northwards out of the Carolinas and into Virginia. Because of this the chastened New Jersey along with the other units stationed near the Hudson, as well as their French allies, were soon to be called upon to march south and take part first in the operations in Virginia, and then in the Yorktown campaign which was to bring the Revolutionary War to its close.

Chapter Ten

THE CAMPAIGNS IN THE CAROLINAS

'Clinton's instructions to Cornwallis included suggestions . . . that assistance should be given in operations to be carried out in Virginia "as soon as we are relieved from our apprehension of a superior fleet and the season will admit".'

The British offensive in the South was an attempt to crush the rebellion by striking in an area where there were a large number of loyalists. Towards the end of 1778 Clinton dispatched 3,500 men by sea from New York to Georgia, and, reinforced by troops from the garrison in the Floridas, they succeeded in seizing Savannah and taking Augusta. In the following year an American army under Benjamin Lincoln was beaten off when attempting to regain Savannah, and after this a firm base was established by the British in the southernmost colony.

In December 1779 Clinton with Cornwallis as his second-in-command sailed from New York at the head of a force of 6,000 men with the intention of trying to capture Charleston in South Carolina, a prize which had eluded the British grasp a few years earlier. Clinton arrived off the coast of the Carolinas in February 1780 and after waiting a few weeks for reinforcements to arrive from Georgia set about seizing the port. A sand bar effectually blocked the entrance to the harbour to larger vessels so Clinton's naval commander Admiral Arbuthnot left his ships of the line outside in the bay and sent in only his frigates. Once across the bar, the little ships faced the guns of Fort Moultrie which dominated the narrow channel to the inner harbour. These guns had halted Admiral Parker earlier, but Arbuthnot boldly ran his frigates past them. Meanwhile the troops had landed, and, after marching inland, had laid out siege parallels across the northern side of the Charleston peninsula, so that the port was successfully surrounded. On 13 April from dominating positions on land and sea the British began their bombardment, subjecting the town to a rain of shell and red-hot shot, which caused a great deal of damage and many casualties. After a week of this, Lincoln decided to ask for terms; but the discussions about conditions, which began on 21 April, dragged on for several weeks, the main point at issue being whether the Americans might be allowed to march out with drums beating and colours unfurled. Eventually on 12 May, influenced no doubt by a renewal of the bombardment, the Americans marched out with their colours cased as the British had all along insisted. Thus the first encounter in the South was an outstanding victory for the British. In addition to 2,500 Continentals some 2,000 militiamen were made prisoner, and substantial stores and great quantities of arms were captured. It was the most serious defeat yet suffered by the Americans during the whole war.

*

After consolidating in Charleston Clinton sent off columns to try and subdue the rest of South Carolina. One of these marched northward with the object of seizing the American post at Ninety-Six, and a larger force under Cornwallis set off to occupy Camden. At this stage the recruitment of loyalists to serve alongside the regulars was put in train, and Major Ferguson was appointed their leader with the title of inspector of militia. After completing these arrangements Clinton took his departure, leaving the pacification of the rest of the South to Cornwallis. His final instructions to the latter included suggestions that a move into North Carolina might be made after dealing with South Carolina, and also that assistance should be given in operations to be carried out in Virginia 'as soon as we are relieved from our apprehension of a superior fleet and the season will admit'. Apart from this, Cornwallis was given full authority. He was empowered to act offensively or defensively as he might choose, to manage all stores and provisions, to give orders to the troops in Georgia and the two Floridas, to issue money, to hold courts-martial, to embody militia, and to organise captures. Except that he had to keep Clinton informed of what he was doing, his command was virtually an independent one.

*

A few weeks later, as Cornwallis's column was approaching Camden, it was learned that far ahead lay a small force of Virginians under Colonel Bufold, who had been delayed on their way to reinforce Charleston. Immediately Tarleton and his British legion were sent forward to give battle, and riding north 150 miles in fifty-four hours, the troopers caught up with the Virginians at Waxhams, half-way between Camden and Charlotte. Representing his force as twice its actual size Tarleton ordered the enemy to surrender. At first they refused to do so, even making as if to fire at the horsemen. Then, too late, they changed their minds. By this time the troopers were galloping forward in a charge and could not be halted. They rode in and butchered most of the force, killing 113 men outright.

This encounter had most unfortunate consequences. News of it spread quickly, and because the troopers appeared to have killed fellow Americans in the act of surrendering, 'Tarleton's Quarter' became a byword throughout the Carolinas. What was worse, it inspired a bitter revenge, and brought to the fighting in the South some of the worst aspects of a civil war.

*

In August 1780, when the British were installed at both Ninety-Six and Camden, it was learned that the victor of Saratoga General Gates was marching south to give battle. At Camden in the direct path of Gates's advance Cornwallis had assembled a quantity of stores and equipment. He also had some 800 of his soldiers sick in hospital in the town. Because of this he did not want to abandon the place to the enemy and retire to the relative safety of Charleston. Instead, he slipped a spy into the enemy to discover their strength with a view to attacking. The man pretended to be a Marylander sympathetic to the patriot cause who was pleased to see so many Marylanders in Gates's train. So plausible was he that the sentries led him to headquarters where he offered to spy on Cornwallis, all the while noting the state of the American force. He fooled Gates completely, and returned with valuable information. Tarleton's scouts had also not remained idle. They managed to capture three enemy soldiers and bring them back mounted behind for Cornwallis to interrogate. The prisoners spoke freely of what they believed were their commander's intentions, and even announced he was about to march on Camden with 5,000 men. Cornwallis had less than 3,000 he could put in the field; but nevertheless decided to advance and attack the Americans at dawn next morning. On the same afternoon Gates had given orders for a night march on Camden. Thus it came about that at precisely the same hour the two forces were marching to meet each other.

The road out of Camden was flat at first, then it dipped sharply to cross Saunders Creek, and finally climbed up again. The British scouts had hardly crossed the creek before they brushed with the advanced troops of the American force. Hearing shots Cornwallis halted the main body and formed them up in line athwart the road. The position was a good one

Banastre Tarleton by Sir Joshua Reynolds (reproduced by courtesy of the Trustees, The National Gallery, London)

with gum swamps protecting both flanks, but night had fallen and, as an assault in the darkness would be a risky undertaking, Cornwallis ordered his men to remain in their battle positions for the night, and be ready to attack at dawn next morning.

Meanwhile, in Gates's headquarters all was confusion. He had expected to surprise the British by falling on them while they were asleep in Camden. Instead he had bumped into them as a formidable fighting formation on the road. At first he could not decide what to do. Eventually, after his colleagues had pointed out there was nothing he could do but fight, he too ordered his army to attack at first light.

*

On 16 August 1780 the day broke hot and hazy, but soon through the mist Cornwallis could see his enemy facing him in a long line across the road, parallel to his own, and only about two hundred and fifty yards away. He noticed that the Continentals were in position on the west of the road and the Virginia militia on the east, and quickly determined to make his main effort against the latter. However, before he could issue the necessary orders the enemy militiamen themselves began to advance in a ragged attack. Colonel Lord Rawdon who commanded the British right seeing the confused mob coming towards him sent in his light infantry with bayonets fixed in a counter-attack. At fifty yards from the enemy they halted and fired a volley. Then they charged. This was too much for the militia most of whom flung down their muskets and fled. Their panic spread to the Carolinians on the right and soon all the units on the east of the road were starting to run away. The Continentals from Delaware and Maryland on the west of the road, however, were stauncher. They stood firm even though Tarleton's horsemen came charging through them. But finally, when struck by the British reserve, they too began to give way. This was despite frantic efforts by their commander de Kalb. When the French general's horse was shot from under him, he got up and fought his way to the front on foot, only to fall mortally stricken with eleven wounds. Inspired by their leader his men fought on for a time, and there followed one of the most violent hand-to-hand clashes of the war; but hemmed in on all sides, outnumbered nearly four to one, and with Tarleton's men charging into them again, the pressure was too strong, and finally the Continentals too turned and ran. Thus in less than an hour Cornwallis shattered the only American army in the South. He also captured considerable booty, including seven cannon, 170 wagons and the many muskets the militia had cast aside in their flight. A feature of the

aftermath was the speed with which the Americans scurried away. Gates
provided an example by riding one hundred and fifty miles and reaching
Hillsboro in three days. Rarely has a general gone so far and so fast after an
unsuccessful battle. The militia fled almost as fast as their leader, and the
Continentals scattered so speedily, and then became so widespread, that
barely seven hundred managed to muster at Hillsboro ten days later.
Tarleton's troopers did much to hasten the departure of Gates's men.
They dealt most ruthlessly with any slow movers, and the road north was
soon strewn with the bodies of those who had been overtaken and killed
by the Legion in their pursuit along with the dead horses, the broken
wagons, the baggage, arms, knapsacks and accoutrements, which form
the trail of all great disasters.

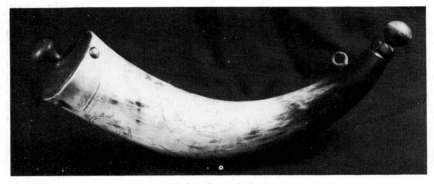

Tarleton's powder horn

*

Following the victory at Camden, Cornwallis quickly consolidated his
hold on South Carolina. Then he took steps, in accordance with his instructions, to carry the war into North Carolina; but owing to difficulties
in acquiring wagons to maintain his army in the field he was not able to
make a move until 8 September 1780, and even then he was further
delayed when fever caused so much sickness in his column that he was
forced to pause for two weeks at Waxhams to allow his invalids to
convalesce.

Cornwallis's first objective was the town of Hillsboro which he
planned to turn into his main base, fed not only by the wagon trail from
Camden but also by river transport up from Wilmington on the coast.
From Hillsboro he hoped to be able to conduct operations throughout
North Carolina, and pacify the colony as he had done South Carolina.

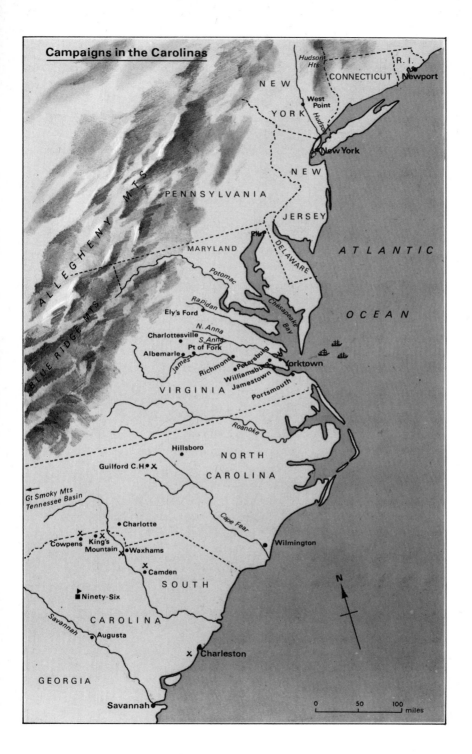

Campaigns in the Carolinas

NEW YORK

Hudson Hts

CONNECTICUT

R. I.
Newport

West Point

Hudson

New York

NEW JERSEY

ATLANTIC

ALLEGHENY MTS

PENNSYLVANIA

MARYLAND

DELAWARE

Phia

Potomac

OCEAN

Chesapeake Bay

BLUE RIDGE MTS

Rapidan

Ely's Ford

N. Anna

Charlottesville

S. Anna

Albemarle

Pt of Fork

James

Richmond

Petersburg

Williamstown

Yorktown

VIRGINIA

Jamestown

Portsmouth

Roanoke

Hillsboro

NORTH CAROLINA

Guilford C.H. X

Gt Smoky Mts
Tennessee Basin

Cape Fear

Charlotte

X X

Cowpens

King's Mountain

X Waxhams

Wilmington

X Camden

SOUTH

Ninety-Six

CAROLINA

Savannah

Augusta

X Charleston

GEORGIA

Savannah

N

0   50   100
miles

While Cornwallis and the main body of the army were plodding slowly north on the Charlotte-Hillsboro road, Ferguson and the loyalist militia were advancing wide on the western flank, scouring the country to raise more loyalist soldiers, and at the same time attempting to scatter any rebels encountered. Unfortunately for Cornwallis this division of his forces, coupled with the impetuosity of his militia leader, was to have unfortunate results and upset his plans.

*

Ferguson began by moving off far and fast towards the north-west. By late September he had reached the foot of the Great Smoky Mountains. There he learnt that some of the men of the upper Tennessee settlements had been intimidating British supporters and harbouring rebel refugees. By a prisoner he sent them a warning to cease hostilities. He threatened that if they did not do so he would march across the mountains and seize and hang their leaders. The reaction of the Tennessee men was to rise in arms. A thousand of them under William Campbell, Isaac Shelby, John Sevier and others later to become renowned, along with some refugees led by Joseph McDowell, moved over the mountains to confront the British leader and his loyalists. Armed with flintlock rifles, tomahawks and scalping knives, with the trappings of their horses stained red and yellow, their fringed hunting skirts girded by bead belts, and their coon-skin caps stuck with bucktails, the mountain men looked a very motley crowd. They were, however, to prove good fighters.

Just before the Tennessee men crossed the Blue Ridge at Gillespie's Gap, two members of Sevier's band deserted and fled to warn Ferguson of the force moving against him. The British leader, realising he was likely to be attacked by a superior force while on his own, immediately sent a call for help to Colonel Cruger at Ninety-Six in his rear, and a message explaining his predicament to Cornwallis who was at Charlotte to the east. Then, having satisfied himself that his colleagues had been informed, he began to take his own evasive action. He feinted first towards Ninety-Six, then he pulled back as if to join the main body at Charlotte. Finally he turned and installed his force on King's Mountain, a stony flat-topped ridge with steep sides clad with trees about half-way between his two colleagues. He manned the whole northern half of the ridge, and apparently felt quite confident when in position, for he declared boldly: 'I am on King's Mountain. I am king of the mountain and God Almighty will not drive me from it.'

Meanwhile, the Tennessee men were hurrying after their quarry. They lost the trail near Cowpens, and a few miles from the crossing over Broad River they went into camp; but a spy reported Ferguson's movements to some local patriots led by Edward Lacy and the latter rode over and told them where their enemy had gone. At a hastily-called council of war it was decided to attack Ferguson without delay, and at sunrise on 7 October they broke camp and were soon splashing through Broad River at Cherokee Ford. Throughout the forenoon it rained steadily, but they pushed on without halting, merely wrapping their long hunting skirts round their rifles to keep them dry. About three o'clock in the afternoon they learnt of Ferguson's exact position from two captured loyalists, and soon afterwards reached King's Mountain and took up position round its base, almost completely surrounding the area which Ferguson's men occupied. They then dismounted, formed two lines, primed their weapons, and prepared to attack.

Ferguson had one hundred troops drawn from the King William American Regiment, the Queen's Rangers and the New Jersey Volunteers, along with a thousand loyalist militia, and he prepared to receive the enemy by placing his men in position behind the slaty ledges around the summit. He was wearing a light-coloured hunting shirt, and carried his sword in his left hand because he had not regained full use of his right after being wounded at Brandywine. Round his neck hung a silver whistle which he used to rally his men. He planned to repulse the enemy by volley firing followed by bayonet charges, methods he had previously found effective.

The battle began when William Campbell's followers stormed up the hill, yelling and firing their rifles. The men on the summit replied with a volley; and then, cheering lustily, they charged and drove the patriots down again. No sooner had they done so, and returned to the summit, than Isaac Shelby's men came swarming up from the other side. All the while Ferguson on horseback rode from point to point encouraging his men with blasts from his whistle; and, by bayonet charges, under his direction, Shelby's men were driven back, and Campbell's again, and then other groups. But in every charge many fell, and finally when ammunition ran short, white flags of surrender began to be raised on the hill. Ferguson rode over and cut down two such flags. Then he rallied a staunch band recruited from the Ninety-Six area and led them forward in a further charge. However, this time Ferguson's light shirt attracted the attention of several patriot sharpshooters, and he had not gone twenty yards before he fell from his horse 'literally shot to pieces'.[1] It was virtually the end of the battle on King's Mountain. After the loss of their leader the whole line round the summit began to crumble, and although Captain de Peyster took over command and staged a rally round the baggage, it was not long before he decided to capitulate.

Three hundred loyalists were killed or wounded on King's Mountain, and half as many Tennessee men; but the worst feature of the battle was its aftermath. Remembering Tarleton's treatment of Bufold's men at Waxhams and his slaughter of Gates's troops fleeing after the battle at Camden, the mountain men cried loud for 'Tarleton's Quarter'. They continued firing after the surrender, and when this butchery ended, they treated their surviving victims with utmost brutality. The wounded men were left unattended, and from among those who marched off as prisoners nine were hanged from a giant oak, watched compulsorily by their fellows. Many died in captivity, and by the end of November of the six hundred taken prisoner only one hundred and fifty remained in rebel hands to be marched away under guard to be confined at Hillsboro.

*

The disaster on King's Mountain resulted in the postponement for the time being of further British operations in North Carolina. It also depressed the loyalists and discouraged them from joining the royal army. However, both Clinton and Cornwallis were convinced that only by an extension of the war could the hold on South Carolina and Georgia be retained, so in January 1781 Clinton sent Leslie with a force of some two thousand men to reinforce Cornwallis and assist him.

Cornwallis had withdrawn to winter quarters in South Carolina after receiving the news of the death of Ferguson and the destruction of his militia; but not before he had made the necessary arrangements for operations to be carried out during the next campaigning season. He despatched a small force to the mouth of the Cape Fear River in North Carolina to open up a supply route up-river to Hillsboro; and he asked Clinton to send forces to Virginia to harass Greene's rear. Then, as soon as Leslie arrived with the reinforcements, he set off again towards North Carolina. Horatio Gates had now been replaced by Nathanael Greene who was a much more competent general; but the campaign that followed closely resembled the previous one in its mixture of failure and success.

---

[1] Recorded in a letter from de Peyster to Cornwallis dated 11 October 1780.

Before Cornwallis's columns had gone far on the road north to Hillsboro which was again chosen as the British forward base, Greene's men in two columns had been put on the move in a contrary direction. Morgan's riflemen along with a few dragoons had as their objective the British post of Ninety-Six, and Greene with the rest of the army was heading towards Camden.

When Cornwallis learnt that Ninety-Six was being threatened he despatched Tarleton's Legion reinforced by the 7th and 71st Regiments to its relief. The rival forces met on 17 January at Cowpens some fifty miles north of the post. By the time Tarleton approached, Morgan had placed his infantry in a good defensive position on the side of a hill with his cavalry out of sight behind. Tarleton was never one to hesitate and as soon as he noticed the enemy in front he gave the order to charge. When the horsemen rode in they were met with a sharp volley and forced to fall back, and in this first assault many officers were killed by American sharpshooters on the look out for their distinctive uniform. Next, to the sound of bagpipes, the 71st Highlanders (Highland Light Infantry) were advanced on the left. They were more successful, driving the American right wing back almost to the cavalry. But then at last the American horsemen were loosed. Led by William Washington they charged round from the rear of the hill on the unsuspecting British. Tarleton's horsemen were very badly shaken by their earlier failure. When called upon to counter-charge, they turned, put spurs to their horses and fled, leaving Tarleton behind engaged in a personal encounter with William Washington. This did not last long, for having put a pistol shot into the flank of Washington's horse, Tarleton too turned and made off. The final result was complete victory for the Americans. Of the thousand men engaged on both sides, most of Tarleton's were killed, wounded or captured, whereas only about one hundred Americans were casualties.

Tarleton's failure at Cowpens was a severe set-back for Cornwallis; but nevertheless it did not delay his advance for long. During the last days of January, he put all his remaining troops into light marching order and having burnt his baggage he pushed forward through drenching rain to try and overtake Greene and Morgan and occupy North Carolina.

His move is interesting because it led indirectly to Yorktown. No one could have dreamed that Cornwallis in the Carolinas and Washington on the Hudson Heights, seven hundred miles apart, with quite different objectives, could within eight months meet face to face midway down the coast to settle the issue. Cornwallis's advance north at the end of January

1781 may thus be said to be the first phase of the Yorktown campaign.

*

When Greene learnt that the British were advancing towards him, he fell back rapidly. After this, night and day the chase continued through North Carolina until Greene skilfully put the river on the border of Virginia between his troops and their pursuers. If Cornwallis now hopefully believed that he had carried out successfully the first phase of his plan, he was soon to be disillusioned, for in the middle of March 1781 Greene recrossed the river and took up a position at Guilford Court House. In the engagement that followed the British were definitely the victors, for the Americans were forced to retreat again; but so great was the British loss in officers and men that Cornwallis's future plan for the occupation of North Carolina were disrupted. Indeed, after a brief stop at Hillsboro in the centre of the colony which he had hoped to make his main base, and from which he might have dominated the colony had his force been larger, he felt compelled to move across to Wilmington on the coast to refit. By rights he should now have retired to South Carolina again. Instead, however, he came to an important decision which was to have a vital effect on the result of the conflict. Abandoning the Carolinas for the time being, he moved directly into Virginia, with the intention of uniting with the troops under Phillips and Arnold that Clinton had earlier sent to operate in his rear, and of renewing operations from a new base on the Chesapeake. Thus evolved the second phase in the Yorktown campaign.

Fight between Colonels Washington and Tarleton by Alonzo Chappel

Chapter Eleven

YORKTOWN

'With Yorktown men looked upon the Revolution as accomplished.'
Henry P. Johnston

Before Cornwallis entered Virginia in May 1781 Clinton had already sent
an expedition there under the turncoat Benedict Arnold. Arnold sailed
from New York on 16 December 1780 and anchored off Jamestown
Island early in January. He marched west and entered and plundered
Richmond and then withdrew right back, crossed the James River and
took up a fortified position at Portsmouth. As the only American troops
in Virginia were a few Continentals and the militia of dubious quality,
Washington decided to dispatch Lafayette and his light infantry to confront the invaders. He also persuaded his French allies to send a small fleet
to blockade the estuaries. This first American counter-operation in Virginia did not achieve very much. A British squadron intercepted the
supporting ships at the entrance of the Chesapeake and in the subsequent
naval action had the advantage. Lafayette had planned to invest Arnold's
force in Portsmouth, but on the receipt of the news of the failure of the
French at sea he marched north instead with the intention of rejoining
Washington.

Lafayette had got no farther than the Head of Elk before it was learnt
that Clinton had sent reinforcements that would bring the British army in
Virginia up to a strength of 3,000. On receipt of this information
Washington ordered Lafayette back again with instructions to try to
build up a sufficient force to resist the invaders. But the French general
found the task of reinforcement of his army difficult. The generals[1] present in the colony were his seniors in rank and had to be approached with
the greatest tact, and the populace was discontented and far from cooperative. The problems he faced because of his paucity of numbers and
shortage of provisions as well as the tactics he employed with such success

[1] Steuben, Mühlenberg and others.

are recorded in his correspondence[1] at the time.

'Were I to fight a battle,' he wrote to Washington, 'I should be cut to pieces, the militia dispersed, and the arms lost. Were I to decline fighting, the country would think itself given up. I am therefore going to skirmish but not to engage too far.'

In a letter to Governor Thomas Jefferson dated 26 June 1781 he says: 'Lord Cornwallis . . . yesterday . . . retired with his main body into Williamsburg. We are pressing his rear with our light parties supported by the army, but his lordship has proceeded so cautiously and so covered his marches with his cavalry that it has been under the circumstances next to impossible to do him injury.'

Lafayette's correspondence constantly stresses the difficulties of maintaining, let alone improving, his strength. In another longer letter to Jefferson he writes:

Many and many men are daily deserting. But it is next to impossibility to take them in their flight through the woods . . . they have no reason to complain; they cannot conceive any; but say they are only engaged for six weeks and the harvest time recalls them home.

On the other hand the time of a great many are daily expiring. No relief comes to them and you might as well stop the flood tide as to stop militia whose times are out. The riflemen too are determined to go and take of their harvest so that I shall be left with the continentals. Under these circumstances it should perhaps be better to go and fight Lord Cornwallis. But exclusive of my daily expectation of general Morgan,[2] however disappointed I may have been to his strength, exclusive of the diminution of force I have already experienced, I confidentially will confess with you that I am terrified at the consequences of a general defeat. You are not stranger to the political state. Everything bears for the present a tolerable peace. New York threatened, Carolina reconquered, Lord Cornwallis pushed into Williamsburg after a long retreat, such is the situation of affairs in America that may be laid before mediators. But should we be beat and should the loss of Virginia follow a defeat, new obstacles will be raised against American independency.

An order to the county lieutenants throughout the state immediately to lend to the army every six-month soldier, and a call of militia to come immediately into the field are steps of an absolute necessity. I think, my dear Sir severe examples ought to be made of county lieutenants who neglect to send either the six-month soldiers or their quota of militia. Unless a large number is immediately joined to us, we must measure back the ground we have obtained over his lordship . . .

I have always the same complaints to make against the commissary department. A letter from you to them threatening the severest punishments in case the army is left in

[1] *Lafayette in Virginia*, unpublished letters, pp 17–21 (Baltimore 1928).

[2] Lafayette had sent a personal plea for help to Morgan who was at home recruiting his strength after Cowpens.

the least want may have a good effect. I wish you will write them I have requested these punishments inflicted the first hour the army wants any kind of provisions . . .

Permit me, my dear Sir, once more to insist upon an immediate call of militia. Both brigades are not quite so large as Mühlenberg's[1] brigade has been and still less are fit for duty . . .

The movements of Cornwallis's army in Virginia closely shadowed by Lafayette's force were widespread and involved from the time when the British army from the South entered the colony and reached Petersburg on 20 May 1781 and joined up with Phillips's force. Soon after his arrival in Virginia, Cornwallis moved forward to drive the French general out of Richmond. He crossed the River James opposite Westover twenty-five miles below the city and then turned westward past Malvern Hill to Whiteoak swamp. Lafayette by this time had retreated north at great speed. Crossing first the South Anna and then the North Anna on 4 June he crossed the Rapidan at Ely's Ford and was out of danger of being over-taken. A part of Cornwallis's army had given chase, but called off the pursuit when they reached the North Anna and realised their quarry had eluded them. Cornwallis next instigated two extended raids into the west of Virginia. At the head of 180 dragoons and seventy mounted infantry Tarleton was sent off in a forced march westwards with the object of des-troying the powder and arms store at Old Albemarle Court House and disturbing the assembly then convened at Charlottesville for concerting measures for the better defence of the State. Tarleton met with some suc-cess in his enterprise. He surprised the Assembly in session on 4 June, seized a number of its members, and all but captured Governor Jefferson. He also destroyed a quantity of the stores he found in the town. About the same time as Tarleton was raiding Charlottesville and Albemarle Court House, Simcoe with a hundred cavalry and three hundred infantry was marching westward along the north bank of the James River towards Point of Fork, thus approaching Albemarle Court House from another direction. Simcoe's raid proved almost as successful as Tarleton's had been. He compelled von Steuben to retreat rapidly from Point of Fork on 5 June and destroyed the large quantity of arms and supplies there. Both raiding columns rejoined Cornwallis and the main army a few miles below Point of Fork on 7 June.

Cornwallis had made two highly successful raids into Virginia, but he nevertheless did not consider his army of 7,000 men strong enough to

[1] Mühlenberg and Steuben were commanders of small bodies of Continentals and larger numbers of militia, and later, along with Wayne, joined up with Lafayette.

General Rochambeau, French
engraving from life portrait

carry out a sustained aggressive campaign to recover Virginia. Consequently he withdrew. Followed by Lafayette's force which had now been joined by von Steuben's and numbered some 4,500 men, he moved eastward, crossed the James River, and established himself at Portsmouth.

Meanwhile, up on the Hudson, the presence nearby at Newport of the well-appointed French army under Rochambeau caused Washington to consider a joint attack on New York, and he rode over to talk with his colleague about the matter. On his arrival for his conference with the French general, he was told that the long-awaited French fleet under Admiral de Grasse had broken through the British cordon off Brest. It was, he was told, already operating in the West Indies and might soon be sailing northward to the waters off the east coast. Rochambeau at once informed his ally that the presence of this fleet, which together with the squadron at Newport would give French command of the sea, would allow him to leave the still-blockaded Newport and make the French army available to operate alongside Washington's.

Washington still considered their best plan would be to make an attack on New York, and on 22 July 1781 a joint demonstration to test the defences was made in front of King's Bridge on the Harlem River. Warned of the attack, Clinton immediately withdrew his advanced troops over the river on to New York Island, and the allies did little more than learn more about the formidable defences in the area.

The assault caused Clinton to order Cornwallis to send 3,000 of his men to reinforce the British garrison of New York. This would have seriously weakened Cornwallis. But Clinton almost immediately had a change of mind and sent the instructions to Cornwallis which were to lead to the encirclement of the whole force at Yorktown. He told his subordinate that he need not after all send the troops to New York if he thought they could be better employed in Virginia. He also suggested that Cornwallis might establish his force in a defensive position either at Old Point Comfort or Yorktown.

On receipt of Clinton's second message it did not take Cornwallis long to decide to avail himself of the option to keep the troops he had designated for New York, and finding that Old Point Comfort was more difficult to defend than Yorktown, he decided to take his army over the James and sail round and occupy the latter place. On their arrival at Yorktown Cornwallis despatched a detachment under Tarleton to occupy Gloucester on the opposite side of the York River. This was to assist his two frigates the *Charon* and the *Guadelöupe* in the guarding of the channel between the two places.

*

The Yorktown campaign opened on 14 August, when Washington received dispatches telling him that Admiral de Grasse had set sail from the West Indies with a substantial fleet and 3,200 troops. His immediate destination it seemed was Chesapeake Bay. As, in view of his other commitments, he could only be in the area for a short while, the French admiral hoped that the plans for any combined naval and land operation contemplated would be made in advance of his arrival.

Rochambeau had always favoured Virginia as the venue for the joint operation, and when Washington heard of the likely presence in the near future of a French fleet off the Virginia Capes he too now believed an advance south to join and reinforce Lafayette's army should be made. Consequently orders were immediately issued for the French army accompanied by a select American force, in all numbering some 8,000 men, to take the road for Virginia.

The march began on 19 August 1781, only four days after the news had been received that de Grasse was on his way. The troops used three separate routes across New Jersey as far as Princeton. This was to confuse Clinton so that he should not fully understand what was happening until the allied army was well on the way. In the event, few even among the allies realised what was afoot. For example, Joseph Trumbull, Washington's secretary, was to write: 'By these manoeuvres, and the correspondent march of the troops, our own army no less than the enemy are completely deceived.'

From Princeton the road to Trenton was taken by all three columns, and from there they marched to the head of Chesapeake Bay where Washington and Rochambeau left them to embark and proceed by ship, while the two commanders rode on overland. Washington's party stopped en route for a few days at Mount Vernon, and Washington had the pleasure of entertaining the French general and the officers of the two staffs in his own home which he had not visited for six years. The party reached Williamsburg on 14 September and from then on Washington assumed overall command of the allied forces.

*

While the allied forces were marching south, there had been important happenings off the coast of Virginia on the approach of de Grasse and his fleet after an undisturbed voyage from Brest via the West Indies.

The senior British naval officer in the area was Admiral Rodney, then in the West Indies, and it was his duty to neutralize the French fleet. As early as 3 May 1781, he had sent a signal to Admiral Arbuthnot at New York telling him to be on his guard 'should they visit the coasts of America'. But Arbuthnot had since gone off home and had been replaced by Graves. When later Rodney heard that de Grasse was heading north from the West Indies he sent a second signal, this time to Graves, saying he was dispatching a squadron north to unite with Graves and asking that a frigate be sent to Chesapeake to meet it. This message never reached Graves. The captain of the sloop-of-war that carried it reached New York safely, and finding Graves away reconnoitring sailed in search of him; but on his way he was overtaken by three American privateers. These forced him to run his vessel aground on Long Island and the dispatches were lost. Meanwhile Rodney, having sent Hood northward with the promised squadron, had gone home to England on sick leave.

From this stage everything went wrong with the British arrangements. Hood with a squadron of fourteen ships of the line, six frigates and one fireship, sailed up the coast and reached the Chesapeake on 25 August. But he found no French vessels in the area—and no frigate from Graves. Continuing his course, he reached Sandy Hook and was at last able to render a report on the situation. This was the first Graves knew of the approach of de Grasse, and realizing the necessity to act at once he joined his ships to Hood's and assuming command of the whole fleet bore down on the Chesapeake. But it was too late. De Grasse had been five days behind Hood sailing up from the West Indies, and the British excursion to New York had enabled him to arrive first at the Chesapeake and get safely ensconced in the bay.

The two fleets hove into sight of each other on 5 September, the day the troops aboard the French transports were in the process of landing on Jamestown Island. De Grasse left the transports to their own devices and slipping the cables of his ships of war stood out to sea to give battle.

In their haste to sail out of the bay the French ships became split up into three groups of eight vessels which in their turn were somewhat separated. Graves seeing the opportunity they presented in their scattered formation immediately ordered his ships to close in on a number of straggling enemy vessels bringing up the rear of de Grasse's line; but his signal being misunderstood, instead of tackling the ships he intended, they sailed in among the leading French men of war. In the encounter that followed the British had the advantage of the wind but this was more than countered by the good gunnery of the French which enabled them to inflict greater damage than they sustained. At dusk de Grasse pulled away to correct his line and the British almost lost contact; but during the night both fleets continued to sail with lights defiantly ablaze just out of range of each other. During the next two days the fleets manoeuvred southward while the damage done in the battle was being repaired. On the third day they were off the coast of North Carolina when a storm arose. This caused such serious leaks in the *Terrible*, which had already been badly battered in the battle, that Graves ordered the vessel to be abandoned and blown up—thus increasing the French advantage. After this the fleets started manoeuvring northward again, during which time de Grasse managed to keep his ships between the British fleet and the entrance to Chesapeake Bay. Meanwhile, as Graves could not see an opportunity of engaging a part of the numerically superior French fleet, he avoided de Grasse's efforts to bring him back to battle.

On 9 September after the fleets had been in some sort of contact for four days, de Grasse sighted sails to the north. Though it was impossible to identify the ships in the distant haze, de Grasse presumed they were part of de Barras's squadron with the siege artillery and supplies on the way from Newport to join him, so he manoeuvred once again to place his fleet between the approaching French ships and the British fleet. It proved indeed to be the French Newport squadron, and protected by de Grasse's skilful move, the ships with the convoy of transports proceeded safely into Chesapeake, thereby adding still more to the advantage the allies had over the British in the area.

During the next night the British fleet disappeared. Graves had set course for New York to repair the damage, and directly de Grasse realized the enemy had gone he returned to his anchorage in Chesapeake Bay. Here, two days later, two enemy frigates were surprised and captured attempting to destroy buoys, and then the famous battle off the Virginia Capes came to an end.

Tactically it ended slightly in favour of the French who were able to claim credit for the destruction of the *Terrible*, the capture of two frigates, and in general more damage done to enemy shipping than their own sustained. Strategically, however, it was the most important battle of the war, for it gave the French command of the sea off Chesapeake Bay and thereby isolated Cornwallis in Yorktown and left him at the mercy of allied armies superior in manpower and equipment.

*

On 18 September Washington visited the French fleet and spent most of the day conferring with Admiral de Grasse in his 120-gun flagship *Ville de France*, the largest warship in the world in her day. Around in the anchorage lay the thirty-one other ships which gave the control of the seas off the bay which Washington had been dreaming of for years.

Although in the dispatches Washington had received from the French admiral he had appeared somewhat demanding, on acquaintance de Grasse proved to be as courteous and cooperative as Rochambeau. Despite an earlier announcement that he would have to leave by the middle of October he readily agreed not only to remain and blockade Yorktown until the end of the month, but also to provide a contingent of marines and sailors as a reinforcement for General St. Simon whose men he had brought from the West Indies. He would not, however, agree to send a squadron up-river to take control of the passage between Yorktown and Gloucester.

Then, just when all seemed settled, news came that Graves had been reinforced by the arrival in New York of another squadron from home, and

Admiral de Grasse, engraving by J. Chapman

de Grasse announced that he was going to sail northward and give battle to the British.

This naturally caused great consternation in the allied camp at Williamsburg. After a brief conference both Washington and Rochambeau sent separate pleas to de Grasse begging him to remain and prevent the relief of Cornwallis. Washington sent Lafayette in person to convey his message. It was perhaps as well for the cause that he did so. At any rate, Lafayette managed to persuade his fellow countryman to remain at anchorage off Yorktown and all was well.

*

Washington next set about preparing the plans for the investment of Yorktown. For the task he had 9,500 Americans, including 3,200 Virginia militia under Governor Thomas Nelson, and Rochambeau's army which with St. Simon's force brought from the West Indies in de Grasse's ships numbered some 7,500 men. With the detachment of marines and sailors provided by de Grasse the entire allied force totalled 18,000. Washington

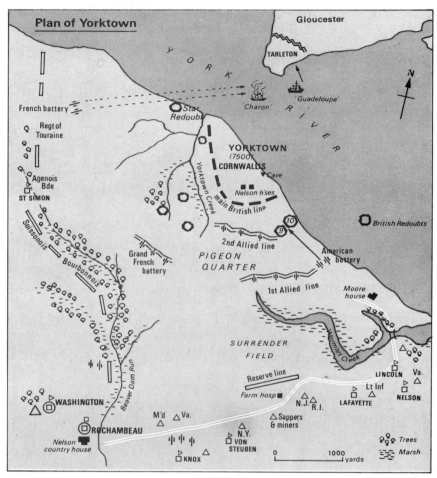

was the supreme commander. Rochambeau led the French wing and Benjamin Lincoln was nominally in charge of the American wing though he also appears as the commander of a division. To oppose this formidable allied force, Cornwallis had 7,000 men in Yorktown and 700 at Gloucester on the other side of York River two miles away. The British force was comprised of two infantry brigades, a brigade of guards, 1,700 Germans, 115 Loyalists, 450 cavalry and 200 artillerymen.[1]

*

Yorktown is situated on a plateau on top of low cliffs bordering the es-

[1] Appendix One gives the complete orders of battle for both sides.

tuary of the York River. In 1781 it was protected on the west by the York-town Creek which was then marshy at its source and possessed a tidal estuary and a ravine at its coastal end. A somewhat similar protection was afforded by Wormley Creek to the south-east. Between the sources of the two creeks was a flat area known as the Pigeon Quarter which was chosen by Washington as his main approach to the fortified township. The banks of the streams appeared to have carried trees in 1781 but from the records there does not appear to have been as much woodland in the area as at the present time.

Before the arrival of the allies before Yorktown, Cornwallis was able to construct an extensive line of fortifications around the town which in-cluded a number of isolated redoubts in advance of the main defences. The three most important of these forward redoubts were the Star or Fusilier redoubt in the north-west by the coast in advance of the York-town Creek estuary, and the redoubts numbered 9 and 10 guarding the coastal approach in the east. The forward redoubts built to the west of Pigeon Quarter in the area of the upper waters of Yorktown Creek were abandoned by the British early on. Cornwallis also fortified and garri-soned Gloucester Point on the other side of the river.

*

On 28 September the allied armies left Williamsburg and marched east-ward towards Yorktown. On approaching the town they formed a line of investment a mile or so away from the main British line of fortifica-tions. The Americans took the right of the line and set up their tents along the track leading to Moore House on the cliffs, with Lincoln's division in the woods by Wormley Creek, and then in succession Nelson's militia, Lafayette's light infantry, and von Steuben's division. The dividing line between the two wings was Beaver Dam Run, a stream running con-veniently from north to south in the centre of the position. Rochambeau's headquarters was in the Nelsons' country house beside the stream, and Washington's in tents just to the west of the French general. The French army went into position along a belt of trees stretching north-west from their headwater near Beaver Dam Run, with the Bourbonnois brigade by the headwaters of the Run followed to the north-west by the Soissonois brigade, and with the Agenois brigade nearest the coast.

*

After a careful reconnaissance of the position Washington decided to make his assault in the sector from the Pigeon Quarter to the coast on the right of the allied line; but the attack could not be staged immediately owing to the time required to haul the siege guns from the landing place at Jamestown and place them in position.

The siege operations were begun by digging the first parallel to west of Moore House and the estuary of Wormley Creek. At dusk on the evening of 6 October 4,000 Americans and Frenchmen paraded and then marched forward to the designated area. Benjamin Lincoln commanded the American detachment and Baron de Viomenil the French. About a third of the troops did the digging while the rest lay under arms to repel attack. The first group were placed by the engineers on arrival along the projected line and set to digging. They worked so silently during that dark night of gentle rain that the British neither heard nor saw what was going on until daybreak. The eight hours' work proved highly satisfactory. Although the trenches were by no means completed, they were nevertheless quite high enough to protect the parties who were to continue the digging the next day.

During the first phase of the siege operations the allies suffered no casualties in the eastern sector where the first parallel was being constructed, but they did have a loss of some twenty men killed or wounded on the extreme left while the Regiment Touraine was staging a noisy demonstration against Star Redoubt in order to take the enemy's attention away from the digging in progress in the east.

For ten days until the closing scene the siege operations proceeded systematically. Von Steuben was the only general officer in the American army with siege experience so was naturally in much demand from those seeking advice on the operations in hand. Henry Knox, who was again in charge of the American artillery, was also to play an outstanding role by making full use of what the set siege offered his guns and gunners. Quickly appreciating the nature of the ground where he was operating, he issued the following order: 'Upon every occasion where it shall be practical, ricochet firing of shot and shells must be practised. This mode [of bouncing them along the ground] has a great superiority over all others, and is much more economical . . .'

As soon as a battery arrived it was placed in position and brought into action. The first to fire was a French battery on the extreme left opposite Star Redoubt. Erected by the Regiment Touraine, it mounted four twelve-pounders and six howitzers and mortars. Its fire forced the frigate *Guadeloupe* to seek the safety of the Gloucester shore. Shortly afterwards an American battery of six eighteen- or twenty-four pounders, two howitzers and four mortars opened on the extreme right. Then more batteries came into action, including the Grand French Battery alongside the first parallel, and the bombardment really got going.

The bombardment of Yorktown which lasted several days was both spectacular and effective. The American surgeon Thacher writes: 'Some of our shells overriding the town are seen to fall in the river and bursting throw up columns of water like the spouting of the monster of the deep' (not all missed—the *Charon* was set on fire by hot shot from the French battery on the extreme left) '. . . the bomb shells from both the besiegers and the besieged are incessantly crossing each other's path in the air. They are clearly visible in the form of a black ball in the day but in the night they appear like fiery meteors with a blazing tail most beautifully brilliant ascending magestically from the mortar to a certain altitude and gradually descending to the spot where they are destined to execute their work of destruction.'

The effectiveness of the bombardment was recorded at the time by Secretary Thomas Nelson. Nelson who was the uncle of Governor Thomas Nelson who commanded the Virginia militia lived in a large house in Yorktown that 'dominated the profile of the town as seen from the right of the American position'. Alongside was the house of Governor Nelson. It is said that when Lafayette was officer of the day he invited Governor Nelson to be present when one of his batteries was to open fire for the first time. Because of his knowledge of his home town, Lafayette said to the Governor: 'To what particular spot would your Excellency direct that we should point the cannon?' 'There,' replied Nelson, 'to that house. It is mine and now that the Secretary's is nearly knocked to pieces is the best one in the town. There you will be almost certain to find Lord Cornwallis and the British headquarters. Fire upon it, my dear marquis, and never spare a particle of my property so long as it affords a comfort or a shelter to the enemies of my country.'[1] Secretary Nelson's house had indeed been badly battered. Because of this, on 10 October the British allowed the old man to proceed to the American lines under a flag of truce. Secretary Nelson reported on his arrival that the bombardment had already done much damage and forced many of the enemy to take shelter under the cliff where Cornwallis had established his headquarters in a cave. On the Gloucester side, Nelson continued, no less than 1,200 horses had been killed by Tarleton's troopers because the animals could not be fed. To some extent the enemy were dispirited but were not unduly worried as a small boat had slipped into the river with assurance that a fleet of thirty

[1] Custis, 336.

ships would arrive in seven days to relieve Cornwallis.

This last piece of information caused Washington to prosecute the siege with more vigor, and on 11 October work on a second parallel closer to the enemy position was begun. The construction of this second parallel was rendered difficult by the two British redoubts, numbered 9 and 10, which occupied the eastern part of its projected line. As soon as the western section of the second parallel was complete, therefore, and a roomy epaulement constructed close to the redoubts from which the attack might be made, the operations for the taking of the two British strong points were set in train—the task of taking Redoubt 9 was assigned to the French, and Redoubt 10 to the Americans. The French storming party of four hundred men led by Colonel Guillaume de Deuxponts was drawn from the Regiments Gatenois and Royal Deuxponts. Just before dusk, on the given signal of six shots in succession, the force advanced in column of platoons. The first fifty chasseurs carried fascines to fill the ditch. A few of the others carried ladders to scale the parapet. When they were about a hundred yards from the strong point a Hessian sentry heard them and cried out: *'Wer da?'* No answer coming, he opened fire. But he could see nothing to aim at in the darkness so his shots went wide. On reaching the abatis around the fort a halt was made to allow the pioneers to cut a passage. Then the chasseurs filled the ditch, dashed across, and set up ladders to climb the parapet. By this time the garrison of the little post had been alerted. But not soon enough to stop the Frenchmen jumping down among them. So spirited was the attack of Deuxponts' men, indeed, that very soon the Hessians were one by one throwing down their arms and offering themselves as prisoners. Thus Redoubt 9 was carried in less than half an hour; but because of the halt while the pioneers cut through the abati which enabled the enemy to spring to arms, the French loss was considerable. Fifteen were killed and seventy-two were wounded. The enemy, however, had eighteen killed and fifty taken prisoner, and had lost their strong point into the bargain.

The American attack on Redoubt 10 was made by a force of similar size composed of troops from Connecticut, New York, Massachusetts and Rhode Island. Its command at first was disputed. Lafayette as chief of the Light Division which was involved had intended the honor for Gimat, lately his aide, who had served in two campaigns with the light infantry with the brevet rank of lieutenant colonel; but on the date concerned Alexander Hamilton was field officer of the day, and he at once protested against Gimat's appointment for command during his tour of duty. Being informed by Lafayette that the assignment had already been made and approved at headquarters, Hamilton wrote a spirited letter to Washington who upon inquiry into the claim decided in favour of Hamilton much to the latter's gratification.

The work to be stormed was somewhat smaller than the one captured by the French, and situated only twenty feet from the cliffs along the shore of the York's estuary. At the given signal, again of six shots, Hamilton and the bulk of the force advanced on the fort from the front while a detachment under John Laurens moved round and approached from the rear. Unlike the French, neither party waited for the pioneers to clear a path. When they reached the abatis they forced their way through and stormed the fort before its defenders realised what was happening. The whole operation took only ten minutes and the American loss was only nine killed and twenty-five wounded.

From the very beginning of the siege Washington had taken personal control of the operations. The journal of more than one American officer records that the first shot was fired by Washington himself, and although this may be apocryphal, he certainly visited Viomenil and heard with approval the details of that officer's preparations for the storming of Redoubt 9; and he rode over to the ground where Lafayette's officers were waiting and made a brief appeal saying the success of the attack on Redoubt 10 depended on them. Now that both redoubts were successfully captured he was one of the first to visit the works, where, under an enemy fire to which he paid little attention, he had no difficulty in deciding with the engineers' aid the positions in which new batteries should be placed alongside the captured redoubts, and the manner in which the redoubts should be included during the extension of the second parallel to the coast.

The erection of these new defence-works so close to the ramparts around the town created a grave situation for Cornwallis and his men. This is indicated by the letter the former wrote to Clinton on 15 October in which he said: 'Last evening the enemy carried two advanced posts on the left by storm and during the night have included them in the second parallel which they are at present busy in perfecting. My situation now becomes very critical . . .'

But although Cornwallis realised he was caught in a trap from which he was unlikely to escape, he nevertheless determined to make one more effort before surrendering. On the night of 15 October he organised a sortie against the centre of the allied line, and on the following night he

set about trying to transfer his troops to Gloucester Point on the opposite side of York River.

The party detailed to make the sortie was led by Colonel Abercrombie and consisted of four hundred men drawn from the Guards, the 80th of Foot and the Light Infantry. Moving out about three o'clock in the morning they first stormed unnoticed into a battery and drove off the guards and spiked four cannon. Then they turned and entered a contiguous emplacement. As they rushed into the second battery, bayonets fixed, they cried, 'What troops?' 'French,' came the answer, whereupon Abercrombie shouted: 'Rush on, my brave boys, and skin the hounds!' The French guards, however, on this occasion proved stauncher. They rallied and counter-charged to cries of 'Vive le Roi', and in the hand-to-hand encounter that followed killed eight of the intruders and took twelve prisoners for a loss of twenty-one men. It had been a gallant attempt by the British; but not in the end a very successful one, for six hours after the sortie ended all the spiked guns were in action again and firing on Yorktown.

The Gloucester side which Cornwallis now sought had not been subjected to such a serious assault as had Yorktown. Early on a French force under General de Choisy had approached, and in a clash with a British foraging party Tarleton had been unhorsed. At the critical moment, however, more British cavalry had appeared on the scene and after a skirmish Tarleton was able to escape on another mount and the French then withdrew. After this initial incident, the British remained behind their defence works and the French formed a ring of investment around them.

On the night of 16 October Cornwallis began to transfer his troops to the Gloucester side with the desperate intention of breaking through Choisy's besiegers there with his whole force, and by rapid marches pushing northward to New York. Although it was a forlorn hope, he considered it deserved a trial, but unfortunately for him, by a quirk of fate, the weather prevented him from carrying it out. At midnight, after only a few had reached the other side, a severe storm arose that prevented any more crossing, and Cornwallis was forced to discontinue the operation.

The situation was now critical. The British force was surrounded, outnumbered and short of ammunition. Cornwallis's report says: 'We at that time could not fire a single gun . . . I therefore propose to capitulate.'

The surrender of Cornwallis at Yorktown by John Trumbull. Washington is on the right

The end came on 17 October 1781. Early in the morning a drummer accompanied by an officer marched to a point on the ramparts nearest to the allied works. When they were in position the officer waved a white handkerchief and the drummer beat a parley. An American immediately left the allied front line and approached the two men on the ramparts. After blindfolding the officer he led him back into the American lines. The officer bore a letter from Cornwallis that read: 'I propose a cessation of hostilities for twenty-four hours and that two officers may be appointed by each side to meet at Mr Moore's house to settle terms for the surrender of the posts of York and Gloucester.'

EPILOGUE

After two days of negotiations by commissioners from both sides at Moore House the terms of the surrender were finally agreed. By them Washington granted the British much the same honours that had been allowed earlier in the war to the American garrison of Charleston. Among other things the British had to march out with colours cased and were not permitted to play either an American or French march. It is a treasured tradition that the British in the event played the old English tune 'The World Turned Upside Down'. If so it was an appropriate choice.

The French and American troops formed up, colours fluttering, on the road across the Pigeon Quarter past the trenches of the parallels. At precisely two o'clock in the afternoon the defeated marched glumly out. As the column passed it was noticeable that the Hessians were as soberly soldierly as ever but that some of the British had had too much to drink. On arrival at the surrender field muskets were flung down in the hope of breaking the locks, until this was stopped. Cornwallis, pleading illness, remained in his quarters in the town, and his place at the head of the surrendering troops was taken by his second-in-command General O'Hara. O'Hara, it appears, first attempted to hand his sword to Rochambeau, but was referred to Washington. Washington, realising he was being approached by only the second-in-command, sent O'Hara to Lincoln, who accepted the sword in token of defeat and surrender and returned it. About 8,000 soldiers and seamen surrendered at Yorktown and during the siege 500 were lost. The American and French casualties totalled some 400 men.

Under the terms arranged at Moore House, Cornwallis and his senior officers, having given their paroles as prisoners, were allowed liberty of movement. Cornwallis was also given full and free use of the sloop *Bonetta*, and he carried off as many Loyalists as possible in it to New York. Meanwhile the rank and file and the junior officers were marched off to prison camps in Maryland and Virginia.

The American units of the allied army started their long march back to the Hudson early in November, but most of the French troops remained in the area until the spring when they departed for Rhode Island. De Grasse's fleet sailed back to the West Indies shortly after the siege was over.

Although the British were never forcibly dislodged from New York, the surrender at Yorktown was the real climax of the war. There, in 1781, the end of the road which the Americans had started off along from Lexington in 1775 was reached. King George was inclined to continue to try and force the colonists into submission. He wished, he said, 'to carry on the war, though the mode of it require alteration'. Opinion in the British Parliament, however, had changed after the disaster at Yorktown. At sessions held in the last months of 1781 the majority for continuing the war showed a marked decline. After the recess, on 22 February 1782, General Conway in the Commons moved an address to the throne in favour of a discontinuation of the war and 'a happy reconciliation with the revolted colonies'. This motion was lost by a single vote, but five days later Conway introduced the subject again before a fuller house and, after the defeat by nineteen votes of the Government's counter motion for adjournment, carried his address to the King without division. Then, on 4 March, another resolution was passed against 'the further prosecution of offensive war on the Continent of North America for the purpose of reducing the revolted Colonies to obedience by force' and peace was assured. On 30 November 1782 the provisional articles were signed by commissioners from both countries, and on 2 September 1783 the definitive treaty formally ending the war was at last ratified.

Appendix One

ORDERS OF BATTLE

ALLIED ARMY BEFORE YORKTOWN
GEORGE WASHINGTON
COMMANDER-IN-CHIEF

AMERICAN WING

CONTINENTALS

★GENERAL GEORGE WASHINGTON, of Virginia

SECRETARY
★*Colonel* Jonathan Trumbull, Jr., of Connecticut

AIDES-DE-CAMP
Lieutenant-colonel Tench Tilghman, of Maryland; *Lieutenant-colonel* David Humphreys, of Connecticut; *Lieutenant-colonel* David Cobb, of Massachusetts; *Lieutenant-colonel* William S. Smith, of New York; ★*Lieutenant-colonel* John Laurens, of South Carolina

ADJUTANT-GENERAL
★*Brigadier-general* Edward Hand, of Pennsylvania

QUARTERMASTER-GENERAL
Colonel Timothy Pickering, of Massachusetts

ASSISTANT QUARTERMASTER-GENERAL
Lieutenant-colonel Henry Dearborn, of New Hampshire

COMMISSARY-GENERAL
Colonel Ephraim Blaine, of Pennsylvania

CHIEF PHYSICIAN AND SURGEON
Doctor James Craik, of Virginia

★ Commanders and units mentioned in text.

CHIEF OF ENGINEERS
Brigadier-general Chevalier Du Portail

SUPERINTENDENT OF MATERIALS IN THE TRENCHES
Colonei Samuel Elbert, of Georgia

Three Battalions

Rank and File

1. {*Colonel* Joseph Vose, of Massachusets. . . } 8 Mass. Companies 250
{*Major* Caleb Gibbs, of Rhode Island . . . }

2.* {*Lieutenant-colonel* Gimat . . . . . . } 5 Conn., 2 Mass., 1 } 250
{*Major* John Palsgrave Wyllys, of Connecticut } R.I. . . . }

3. {*Lieutenant-colonel* Francis Barber, of New Jersey } 5 N. H., N. J., & c. 200
{*Major* Joseph R. Reid [of Hazen's] . . . }

SECOND BRIGADE
*BREVET BRIGADIER-GENERAL MOSES HAZEN, of Canada
Brigade Major, Captain Leonard Bleeker, First New York

Four Battalions

1. {*Lieutenant-colonel* Ebenezer Huntington, of Conn. } 4 Mass., Conn. 200
{*Major* Nathan Rice, of Massachusetts . . . }

2.* {*Lieutenant-colonel* Alexander Hamilton, of N.Y. } 2 N.Y., 2 Conn. 200
{*Major* Nicholas Fish, of New York . . . . }

3.* {*Lieutenant-colonel* John Laurens, of South Carolina } 4 N.H., Mass., 200
{*Major* John N. Cumming, of New Jersey . . } Conn.

4. {*Lieutenant-colonel* Edward Antill . . . . . } Hazen's Canadian 200
{*Major* Tarleton Woodson . . . . } Regiment

LINCOLN'S DIVISION
*MAJOR-GENERAL BENJAMIN LINCOLN, of Massachusetts
Division Inspector, Major ——— ———

CLINTON'S BRIGADE
BRIGADIER-GENERAL JAMES CLINTON, of New York
Brigade Major, Captain Aaron Aorson, First New York

First Regiment, New York {*Colonel* Goose Van Schaick . . . . } 325
{*Lieutenant-colonel* Cornelius Van Dyke. }
{*Major* John Graham . . . . . }

* Commanders and units mentioned in text.

Rank and
File

Second Regiment, New York {
Colonel Philip Van Cortlandt . . .
Lieutenant-colonel Robert Cochran . .
Major Nicholas Fish (with Light Infantry)
} 350

ARTILLERY BRIGADE
*Brigadier-general HENRY KNOX, of Massachusetts

Second Regiment
[N.Y. & Conn.] {
Colonel John Lamb, of New York . . . . .
Lieutenant-colonel Ebenezer Stevens, of Massachusetts
Major Sebastian Bauman, of New York . . .
} 225

Detachments {
First Regiment
Lieutenant-colonel Edward Carrington, } of Virginia . . 25
Captain Whitehead Coleman . .

Fourth Regiment
Captains Patrick Duffy, William } of Pennsylvania . 60
Ferguson, and James Smith . .
}

CAVALRY
Fourth Regiment Dragoons—*Colonel* Stephen Moylan, of Pennsylvania 60
Armand's Legion 40

INFANTRY
Lafayette's Division—Light Infantry
*Major-general MARQUIS DE LAFAYETTE
Division Inspector, Major William Barber, of New Jersey

First Brigade
*Brigadier-general PETER MUHLENBERG, of Virginia
Brigade Major, Captain John Hobby, Tenth Massachusetts

Dayton's Brigade
Colonel ELIAS DAYTON, of New Jersey
Brigade Major, Captain Richard Cox, First New Jersey

First and Second New
Jersey Regiments
(united) . . . {
Colonel Mathias Ogden . . . . . .
Lieutenant-colonel William De Hart . . .
Major John Hollinshead . . . . . .
} 600

* Commanders and units mentioned in text.

Rank and
File

Rhode Island ． ． | *Lieutenant-colonel Com'dant* Jeremiah Olney ．
Regiment ． ． ． | *Major* Coggeshall Olney ． ． ． ． ． ． } 450
| *Major* John S. Dexter ． ． ． ． ． ．

STEUBEN'S DIVISION
★MAJOR-GENERAL BARON STEUBEN
Division Inspector, Major Galvan

WAYNE'S BRIGADE
★BRIGADIER-GENERAL ANTHONY WAYNE, of Pennsylvania
Brigade Major, Lieutenant Richard Fullerton, of Pennsylvania

First Battalion, Pennsylvania | *Colonel* Walter Stewart ． ． ． ．
| *Major* James Hamilton ． ． ． } 275
| *Major* William Alexander ． ． ． ．
Second Battalion, Penn. ． | *Colonel* Richard Butler ． ． ． ．
| *Lieutenant-colonel* Josiah Harmer ． ． } 275
| *Major* Evan Edwards ． ． ． ．
Virginia Battalion ． ． | *Lieutenant-colonel* Thomas Gaskins ． ． 350

GIST'S BRIGADE
BRIGADIER-GENERAL MORDECAI GIST, of Maryland
Brigade Major, Captain Lilburn Williams, Third Maryland

Third Regiment, Maryland ． | *Lieutenant-colonel Com'dant* Peter Adams 550
Fourth Regiment, Maryland． | *Major* Alexander Roxburg ． ． ． ． 450

SAPPERS AND MINERS
Captain James Gilliland, New York． ． ． ． ． ． ． ．
Captain David Bushnell, Connecticut ． ． ． ． ． ． } 50
Captain-lieutenant David Kirkpatrick, New Jersey(?) ． ． ． ．
Delaware Recruits ． ． ． ． *Captain* William McKennan． ． 60

MILITIA
★GENERAL THOMAS NELSON, Governor of Virginia
BRIGADES
BRIGADIER-GENERAL GEORGE WEEDON ． ． ． ． ． ． 1500
BRIGADIER-GENERAL ROBERT LAWSON ． ． ． ． ． ． 750
BRIGADIER-GENERAL EDWARD STEVENS ． ． ． ． ． ． 750
State Regiment ． ． ． ． ． *Lieutenant-colonel* Dabney ． ． ． 200

★ Commanders and units mentioned in text.

FRENCH WING
★Lieutenant-general COUNT DE ROCHAMBEAU

Aides-de-camp
Count de Fersen; Marquis de Vauban; Marquis de Damas; Chevalier de Lameth; M. Dumas; De Lauberdière; Baron de Clozen

Marechaux-de-camp
★Major-general Baron de Viomenil; *Major-general* Marquis de St Simon; *Major-general* Viscount de Viomenil; *Major-general* Chevalier de Chastellux. ★M. de Choisy, Brigadier-general

Intendant
M. de Tarlè

Quartermaster-general
M. de Béville

Commissary-general
Claude Blanchard

Medical Department
M. de Coste, Physician-in-chief; M. Robillard, Surgeon-in-chief; M. de Mars, Superintendent of Hospitals

Engineers
Colonel Desandrouins; *Lieutenant-colonel* de Querenet; *Major* de Palys; and nine line-officers

ARTILLERY
	Rank and File
Colonel Commandant d'Aboville; *Adjutant* Manduit. Director of the Park, M. Nadal	600

CAVALRY
| Lauzun's Legion, or Volunteers | Duke de Lauzun . . . . | 600 |
| | Count Arthur Dillon . . . . | |

INFANTRY
★Brigade Bourbonnois
Regiment Bourbonnois	*Colonel* Marquis de Laval	900
	Second-colonel Vicomte de Rochambeau	
	Lieutenant-colonel de Bressolles . . .	
	Major de Gambs	

★ Commanders and units mentioned in text.

Rank and
File

*Regiment Royal Deux-ponts
- *Colonel* Count de Deuxponts . . .
- ★*Second-colonel* Count Guillaume de Deuxponts . . . .
- *Lieutenant-colonel* Baron d'Ezbeck . .
- *Major* Desprez . . . . . .

9000

★BRIGADE SOISSONOIS

Regiment Soissonois
- *Colonel* Marquis de St. Maime . . .
- *Second-colonel* Vicomte de Noailles .
- *Lieutenant-colonel* d'Anselme . . .
- *Major* d'Espeyron . . . . . .

900

Regiment Saintonge
- *Colonel* Marquis de Custine. . . .
- *Second-colonel* Count de Charlus . .
- *Lieutenant-colonel* de la Vatelle . . .
- *Major* M. Fleury . . . . . .

900

★BRIGADE AGENOIS

Regiment Agenois . . .
- *Colonel* Marquis d'Audechamp . .
- *Lieutenant-colonel* Chevalier Cadignau .
- *Major* Pandin de Beauregard . . .

1000

*Regiment Gatenois . .
- *Colonel* Marquis de Rostaing . . .
- *Lieutenant-colonel* de l'Estrade . . .
- *Major* de Tourville . . . .

1000

*Regiment Touraine (not brigaded) . . . . .
- *Colonel* Vicomte de Pondeux . . .
- *Lieutenant-colonel* de Montlezun . .
- *Major* de Ménonville . . . . .

1000

BRITISH ARMY

★LIEUTENANT-GENERAL EARL CHARLES CORNWALLIS

AIDES-DE-CAMP
Lieutenant-colonel Lord Chewton; *Major* Alexander Ross; *Major* Charles Cochrane, Acting Aide

DEPUTY ADJUTANT-GENERAL
Major John Despard

★ Commanders and units mentioned in text.

COMMISSARY
—— Perkins

DEPUTY QUARTERMASTER-GENERAL
Major Richard England

DEPUTY QUARTERMASTER-GENERAL'S ASSISTANTS
Captain Campbell, *Captain* Vallancy, *Lieutenant* Oldfield, and *Ensign* St. John

MAJORS OF BRIGADE
Edward Brabazon, —— Manley, J. Baillie, Francis Richardson

ENGINEERS
Lieutenant Alexander Sutherland, commanding; *Lieutenants* Haldane and Stratton

ROYAL ARTILLERY

	Rank and File
Captain George Rochfort, commanding . . . . ⎫	
Captain-lieutenant Edward Fage . . . . ⎭	193

CAVALRY

Queen's Rangers—*★Lieutenant-colonel* J. Graves Simcoe	248
British Legion—*★Lieutenant-colonel* Banastre Tarleton	192

INFANTRY

★BRIGADE OF GUARDS

★BRIGADIER-GENERAL CHARLES O'HARA	467

★LIGHT INFANTRY

★Lieutenant-colonel Robert Abercrombie . . . . ⎫	
Major Thomas Armstrong . . . . ⎭	594

LIEUTENANT-COLONEL YORKE'S BRIGADE

Seventeenth—*Lieutenant-colonel* Henry Johnson	205
Twenty-third—*Captain* Apthorpe(?)	205
Thirty-third—*Lieutenant-colonel* John Yorke	225
Seventy-first ⎧ *Lieutenant-colonel* Duncan McPherson . . . . . ⎫	
⎨ *Major* Patrick Campbell . . . . ⎬	242
⎩ *Major* James Campbell . . . . ⎭	

★ Commanders and units mentioned in text.

Rank and
File

⋆ Commanders and units mentioned in text.

Appendix Two

THE PURPLE HEART

In 1782 George Washington established a badge of military merit to be given to enlisted men and NCOs who displayed 'unusual gallantry or extraordinary fidelity'.

The badge consisted of a heart of purple cloth with a narrow binding, and was sewn on the left breast of the uniform.

One of the first awards was to Sergeant William Brown of the 5th Connecticut for his bravery, the previous year, when storming Redoubt 10 at Yorktown.

Very few purple hearts appear to have been actually presented—only three are recorded—and its bestowal seems soon to have fallen into disuse; but it was revived in 1932 as an award for those wounded in action.

In its modern form the purple heart consists of a medal with Washington's profile on it with a ribbon of purple with white edges.

SELECT BIBLIOGRAPHY

Archives, Letters, Documents and Papers, Newspapers

Braddock E.	*Letters from America* (Brit Museum)
Cadwalader J.	*Military Papers* (PM HB XXXII 1908)
Clinton H.	*Papers* (Clements Library)
Connecticut Courant	
Force P. (ed.)	American Archives 4th Series (Washington 1848)
Gates *Papers*	(NYHS)
Greene *Papers*	(Clements Library)
Jefferson *Papers*	(Princeton Univ)
Jordan J. W.	*Continental Hospitals Returns* (PHMB XXIII 1899)
Knox J.	*Papers* (MHS)
Laurens J.	*Letters* (NYPL)
Lee *Papers*	(NYHS)
Maryland Gazette	
Massachusetts Revolutionary Archives	
Montrésor J. *Journal*	(PHMB VI 1883)
New Jersey Archives	
New Jersey Gazette	
New York Royal American Gazette	
Newport Mercury	
Orme R. Journal	(Brit Museum)
Pennsylvania Archives	
Pennsylvania Evening Post	
Pennsylvania Gazette	
Pennsylvania Packet	
Pennsylvania Ledger	
Rochambeau *Papers*	(L of C)
Schuyler *Papers*	(NYPL)
Steuben *Papers*	(NYHS)
Waldo A. *Diary*	(Penn M H B XXI 1897)
Washington	*Journals* 1748 and later (L of C)
Letters 1747–58	(L of C)
Military Papers 1754–58	(L of C)
Papers	(L of C and Huntington Library LA)
Wayne *Papers*	(PHS)

BOOKS etc

André J.	*Army Correspondence in the Years 1777–8* (New York 1857)
Bancroft G.	*A History of the United States* (Boston 1878)
Barton J. A.	*Lexington: the end of a myth* (History Today 1959)
Bill A. H.	*Valley Forge* (New York 1952)
Bliven B. Jr.	*Battle for Manhattan* (New York 1955)

Boudinot E.	*Journal* (Philada 1894)
Brick J.	*They Fought for New York* (New York 1965)
Burnett E. C.	*The Continental Congress* (New York 1941)
	Letters of the Members of the Continental Congress 8 vols (Library of Congress)
Butcher H. B.	*The Battle of Trenton* (Princeton 1934)
Chidsey D. B.	*The Siege of Boston* (New York 1966)
	Valley Forge (New York 1959)
	The Great Separation (New York 1965)
	Victory at Yorktown (New York 1962)
Cleland H.	*Washington and the Ohio Valley* (Pittsburg 1955)
Clinton H. ed. W. B. Wilcox	*The American Rebellion* (New Haven 1954)
Congress	*Journal of* (Washington D C 1921)
	Letters of (Washington D C 1921)
	Secret Journals of Acts and Proceedings (Boston 1921)
De Puy H. W.	*Ethan Allen and the Green Mountain Heroes* (New York reprint 1976)
Douglas R. B. (ed.)	*A French Volunteer of the War of Independence Pontigaud* (New York reprint 1969)
Dupuy R. E. and T. N.	*The Compact History of the Revolutionary War* (New York 1963)
Essame H.	*A Redcoat Surgeon's Account of 1776* (Military Review 1962)
Ewing G.	*Military Journal* (Yorkers 1928)
Falkner L.	*The Forge of Liberty* (New York 1959)
Feltman W.	*Journal* (New York reprint 1969)
Flexner J. T.	*The Traitor and the Spy* (New York 1953)
Ford W. C. (ed.)	*The Writings of George Washington* (New York and London 1890)
Fortescue Hon. J. W.	*A History of the British Army* vol 3 (London 1902)
Freeman D. S.	*George Washington* 7 vols (New York 1948–58)
French A.	*The Colonials* (New York 1902)
	The Day of Concord and Lexington (Boston 1925)
	The First Year of the American Revolution (Boston 1934)
	George Gage's Informers (Michigan 1932)
	The Siege of Boston (New York 1911)
Greene N. ed. C. Caldwell	*Memoirs* (Philadelphia 1819)
Hatch C. E. Jr.	*Yorktown* (Nat Park Series—Washington D C 1954)
Hatch L. C.	*The Admin of the American Rev. Army* (New York 1904)
Hersey F. W. C.	*Heroes of the Battle Road* (Boston 1930—W Concord 1972)
Johnston H. P.	*The Yorktown Campaign* (New York 1881—reprint 1958)
Ketchum R. M.	*The Battle of Bunker Hill* (New York 1962)
Kinnaird C.	*George Washington* (New York 1967)
Lafayette Marquis de	*Memoirs* (New York 1837)
	Letters to Washington (New York 1944)
	in Virginia—Letters (Baltimore 1928)
	Memoirs, Correspondence and Manuscripts (London 1837)

Lamb R.	*Journal of Occurrences during the American War* (Dublin 1809—reprint New York 1968)
Larrabie H. A.	*Decision at the Chesapeake* (London 1965)
Lee H.	*Memoirs of the War in the Southern Department* (Washington 1827)
Long Island Hist Socy Vol II	*Authentic Documents* (Brooklyn 1869)
Mackenzie C. ed. A. French	*A British Fusilier in Revy Boston* (Harvard 1926—reprint New York 1969)
Martyn C.	*The Life of Artemas Ward* (New York 1926)
Montrésor Journals ed. G. D. Scull	(New York 1882)
Mühlenberg H. M.	*Journals* (Philada 1945)
Paine L.	*Benedict Arnold* (London 1965)
Partridge B.	*Sir Billy Howe* (London 1932)
Peckham H. S.	*Lexington* (Lexington 1971)
Reed J. F.	*Campaign to Valley Forge* (Philadelphia 1965)
Reed J.	*Life and Correspondence* (Philada 1847)
Reed W. B.	*Life and Correspondence of Joseph Reed* 2 vols (Philadelphia 1847)
Riling J. R.	*Baron von Steuben and his Regulations* (reprint Philadelphia 1966)
Rochambeau Conte de	*Mémoires* (Paris 1809)
Smith S. S.	*The Battle of Trenton* (Monmouth Beach N J 1965)
Steuben F. W. von	*Regulations* (Albany 1803—reprint 1952)
Stoudt J. J.	*Ordeal at Valley Forge* (Philadelphia 1963)
Thacher J.	*Military Journal* (Boston 1823)
Tilghman	*Memoirs, Journals and Letters* (Albany 1876)
Tozzi M. D. and Muehleck R. B.	*The Second Battle of Trenton* (Military Review, Fort Leavenworth 1963)
Trevelyan G. A.	*The American Revolution* 4 vols (London 1905–12)
Vall R. W. G.	*The Revolutionary Diary of Lieut Obadiah Gore Jr* (New York 1929)
Vivian F.	*A Defence of Sir William Howe* (Journal of the Society of Army Hist Research—London 1966)
Waldick P. ed. M. D. Learned	*Diary of the American Revolution* (Philada 1907)
Ware T. A.	*Revolution in the Hudson Highlands* (New York 1965)
Washington G. ed. J. G. Fitzpatrick	*The Writings of George Washington 1745–99* (Washington D C 1931–44)
Weig J.	*Morristown* (Nat Park Service Washington 1950)
Weller J.	*The Guns of Destiny—Trenton and Princeton* (Mil Affairs Washington D C 1951)
Wickwire F. B. and M. B.	*Cornwallis and the War of Independence* (London 1971)
Wildes H. E.	*Valley Forge* (New York 1938)
Willard M. W. (ed.)	*Letters of the American Revolution* (Port Washington reprint 1968)

INDEX